PSYCHOLOGY

Essays Practicals & Statistics

A Guide for Students

Murray Morison

Senior Lecturer in Psychology
Hertfordshire Regional College

 LONGMAN

Addison Wesley Longman Limited
*Edinburgh Gate, Burnt Mill, Harlow, Essex, CM20 2JE, England
and Associated Companies throughout the World.*

© Addison Wesley Longman Limited 1996

First published 1990
Revised edition published 1996
ISBN 0582 28810 X

*Produced by Longman Singapore Publishers Pte Ltd
Printed in Singapore*

The publisher's policy is to use paper manufactured from
sustainable forests.

Contents

Acknowledgements

This book has been the outcome of teaching Psychology at A level for 15 years and I am grateful to my students, who have contributed most considerably to my understanding of the subject. In particular I wish to thank Jennifer Gunn, Samantha Harding and Georgina Meikle for permission to publish their essays. I also wish to thank Mark Stevenson for letting me reproduce one of his practical reports. I would like to acknowledge the ideas of Annabel Jeremiah and Emma Warren, which helped me with the practical on feedback, and also my colleague Fatima Bhanji, who provided the original concept. For the excellent revision diagram on perception, I am indebted to Georgina Baxter.

I wish most particular to thank Mary Tappenden who gave me invaluable advice on the development of the statistical section. Her enthusiasm and promptness of response was most welcome. I am grateful to Sue Maunder who kindly looked through all the details of the statistical procedures. Her fine tooth comb was much appreciated. Finally, I would like to extend thanks to Dax Osbourne who provided the excellent cartoons to accompany the statistical section. All the essay titles with dates were set in that year by the AEB. We are grateful for permission to use them. Any answers or suggestions about answers are the sole responsibility of the author.

Preface

This book has been written for GCE A-level students, although it will be of use to other students following introductory courses in Psychology. My experience has been that students do not find it easy initially to write essays at this level. This is likely to be increasingly the case with the transition from GCSE work to A-level work. The aim of this book is threefold. First, it provides students with useful and flexible techniques in essay writing. It needs to be stated clearly here, that this is not a model answer book. Such books give the impression that there is only one 'right' answer; they do not tend to show how essays are actually constructed. Second, it provides guidance into how to choose, plan and execute psychology practicals. Third, it gives an overview of the main statistical procedures that are applicable at this level of work.

The approach in this book is to analyse questions in such a way that the student is provided with a basic framework for an answer. This can be developed into a full essay. The preparation for essays, writing essays for homework and also under test conditions, are dealt with, as are questions of revision and dealing with examinations.

Suggestions for practicals are given. A detailed guide to planning and writing up practicals is provided, along with examples of actual student practicals fully written up and annotated.

A complete guide to statistics is given, with simple to follow step-by-step instructions. In addition to providing students with an introduction to the main statistical procedures, there are examples of questions on statistics and methodology.

To avoid cluttering up the text with footnotes, full references are not given on authors whose work can be readily located in the major text books.

Introduction

In order to complete your course in Psychology successfully, you will have to develop two distinct skills. The first is to be able to write essays on given topics, under time pressure. The second is to carry out a number of practical studies and to write them up in an appropriate manner. In order to undertake practical work effectively, you will also need to develop some facility with statistics. This book is designed to help you develop these skills.

Many students fail to do justice to themselves by a lack of essay writing skills and poor examination technique. While this guide includes a number of specific essays, its purpose is not to provide 'right answers'. Rather, it will show how to prepare for and effectively answer examination questions. Two basic techniques are used with regard to the essays. The first is to provide some examples of essays written by students under test conditions. Generally these are of a high standard, and show what can be achieved. These essays are annotated with comments to highlight their particular strengths and weaknesses. The second approach is to take actual A level questions and to try to show in a visual way the relationship between the various arguments suggested by each question. To do this, 'thought-webs' or 'mind-maps' are used. Students have found this a very flexible way of setting out ideas, which helps them to structure their arguments in the answer.

A wide range of questions has been chosen to touch on most aspects of an introductory course. While no book of this length can be fully comprehensive, most of the major issues in psychology are considered.

The answers given in this book to questions are just suggestions. There are many ways in which questions can be answered. What this book seeks to demonstrate are some of the techniques behind the construction of good answers.

With regard to practical work, this book seeks to make explicit the relationship between the design of an experiment, the type of data generated and the statistical procedures that are then necessary. Guidance is given in the special style of writing that is appropriate for practical work. Particular attention is given to the problem of undertaking observation studies, and how data from such studies should be recorded and presented.

Using the book

Firstly, with regard to essays, study the questions in the area that you are dealing with. When you are set an essay, follow the guidelines that are set out in the next section on the research and planning for essays. Practise making detailed plans before you start writing. This cannot be emphasised enough. In carefully thinking through a plan you deepen your understanding of an issue and it becomes both easier to write about and more memorable. The thought-web approach to planning is particularly helpful, as it enables you to overview at a glance the relationship between all the arguments you will be presenting. It is also a technique that is a considerable aid when it comes to revision.

Study the full-length essays that have been included, to see the way in which the writers have structured their ideas and linked them to the question. Try to incorporate any good points of technique in your own essays.

When the exam approaches then this book can be used as an aid in revision. You can use the questions to practise exam-length essays which can be checked against the detailed plans provided.

Secondly, for practical work, this book provides step-by-step guidance in planning practicals. If this is followed, then the writing up of the practical report will be made relatively easy. Most of the main concepts that involve statistics are covered, and a chart is provided to assist with choosing the most appropriate statistical test. There are also detailed guidance notes on how practicals can be written up.

Again, study the full-length examples that are given, and make a note of any points of good practice that you can incorporate into your own work.

Thirdly, this book aims to provide you with an easy-to-follow explanation of statistics. You will find a step-by-step approach to all the tests you will need. The statistical tables have clear instructions also, to help you use them. The main concepts that you will need to grasp for this part of your course are presented with a range of examples. You will also find various techniques for presenting your data in an interesting way.

The cartoons and diagrams given in the practical and statistical sections are designed to illustrate some of the fundamental concepts. Try to grasp their significance. If you can understand these basic building blocks of the statistical method early in your course, then you will find that statistics are much more straightforward than they may appear at first.

Research for essays and practicals

Your success in the A-level examination will depend upon how effectively you can answer the questions that are set. Your ability to do this will depend on how well you have prepared yourself over the two years of your course. Essays that have been well researched will deepen your understanding of Psychology and provide good material to revise from.

Good practicals also require sound research skills. It is necessary to gather relevant material to provide the background to the research you are doing, and also to provide a clear context for your study. Being methodical and accurate in this work, and developing the ability to summarise well, will be of considerable value to you in this field as well as others.

Research

If you are preparing for a specific essay title, or if you are researching a particular problem relating to practical work, then make sure that you understand the implications of what you are looking into before you start your research. You need to 'decode' essay questions sufficiently to make sure that your research is on the right lines. Similarly, with practicals, you need to be sure that you gather material which relates to the variables that you are considering. For example, if you are comparing arts and science students, then you will need to look for material that is relevant to the study of arts and science, as variables. If you can find no material, then you may need to reformulate your study. It is important that your practicals are related – at least to a significant degree – to recognised psychological research.

Use of texts

There are a considerable number of texts that you may have access to. You will not have time to read all the material in all of them. Make good use of the table of contents and the index in order to find the relevant pages for your particular field of interest. Skim through unfamiliar material, first to get an overview of what is being said, and second to locate parts that are of particular relevance to your needs. Make brief notes *in your own words*. Do not copy verbatim out of the texts. If you rephrase in your own words, you have to think about what you are reading. This will tend to deepen your understanding – and you will use the material more effectively in your essays and practicals. Make sure that you record the important details (names, dates, statistics).

Use of other books

You may find specialist books on specific topics in the library. Try not to get lost in detail, but use these books to provide fuller information on aspects of the essay or practical that you are doing. Again the index and contents pages will prove invaluable for saving time. It is important that you go beyond the one or two main textbooks that you use in order to do well in the final examination.

References

For your essays you should give references. You should mention the books you have referred to. For example:

Gross R. (1992) *Psychology: The Science of Mind and Behaviour,* Hodder and Stoughton

For your practical work the references you give will need to be fuller. You need to show quite clearly where you have gathered your information. You will also need to give details of the sources of the different studies that you mention. You will probably not have actually referred to the actual sources, but you will find the information listed at the back of the textbooks that you use. For example, for a practical on perception, using a textbook by Sdorow:

Beatty J. (1982) 'Task evoked pupillary responses, processing load and the structure of processing resources', *Psychological Bulletin, 91,* pp. 276–9
Chen D. M. *et al.* (1984) 'The ultraviolet receptor of bird retinas', *Science, 225,* pp. 337–40
Newman and Hartline (1982) 'The infrared "vision" of snakes', *Scientific American,* pp. 116–24
Riggs (1985) 'Sensory processes: vision'. In G.A. Kimble and J. Schlesinger (eds.) *Topics in the History of Psychology* (Vol. 1, pp. 165–220) Hillsdale, NJ: Erlbaum.

Sdorow L. M. (1995) *Psychology,* Brown and Benchmark

← This is the text-book from which you have taken the references given above

If you use other sources of information, like CD ROMS or newspapers, then these should also be listed in your reference section.

Other sources

You should look out for programmes on television that are relevant to the field of psychology. They are not uncommon and will often prove highly informative. For programmes that are clearly of relevance to you, it is helpful if you make a few notes and record the main names.

Many libraries now have CD ROM players. CDs of back editions of newspapers like the *Independent* and the *Guardian,* and especially

New Scientist have many articles that may provide up-to-date information on aspects of psychology. There are also some specialist CD ROMs for psychology to which your library may have access.

Making sense of other people's writing

As a student of psychology you will have to spend a lot of time trying to master other people's arguments. These will be set out with greater or less clarity in textbooks, articles, handouts and similar sources. The writing you will be considering will often present conflicting theories and supporting research. It can be quite a task to tease out the various strands of what is being said. It can also be hard to know what is really of importance, which you need to make a note of, and what you can safely leave to one side.

You will probably find that the following methods of working with text help in aiding understanding and in supporting your writing of essays and reports. Some of the ideas presented below are suggested in a Schools Council book, *Learning from the Written Word*, by Eric Lunzer and Keith Gardner (1982).

Analysing

What is the author trying to say? To find out you need to develop skills in analysing text. Material written for A level and beyond can be quite demanding. You need to be able to separate out what is essential from what is merely illustration or commentary. In particular, you need to bring into sharp focus the arguments that are being presented and how they relate to each other. The following techniques are helpful in making sense of a part of a textbook or a long handout. In this approach, you do not just start at the beginning of a piece of writing about psychology, make notes and plough on gradually towards the end. This often means that at no point do you really understand what you are making notes about. The stages suggested below should help you gradually to understand the text you are studying and ensure that your notes are both relevant and useful.

These stages require you to be quite active in understanding the text. At the end of this process you should remember better what you have studied than you would have done by working through the material once, making notes as you go.

Highlighting

The first step is to skim read the whole section that you are going to study, looking briefly at headings and sub-headings to get a complete overview. Then, taking each paragraph in turn, pick out the key phrase or sentence. In a well-written piece, a paragraph will usually have a key point that is then developed. Sometimes there will be two. At this point there is no need to study the text closely. Work quite fast.

If you are studying a handout or your own book, then use a highlighter pen to emphasise a key point. (If you are working with a library book, then jot down a few words to sum up the key phrase. With the steps suggested below make the analytical notes on a separate sheet of paper.)

Dividing

You will sometimes find paragraphs that have more than one argument or proposition that is being developed. Mark the place where the argument switches or shifts, with an oblique line.

Labelling

Now go through the material again, decide what each section is about and put very brief notes in the margin. You will be labelling paragraphs and, where you have put in a division, parts of paragraphs.

Classifying

Now that you have labelled the paragraphs and, in some cases, parts of paragraphs, you can decide on their relative importance. Some paragraphs are crucial to the argument. Others are merely illustrations, examples or further detail. Mark the paragraphs that are key steps in the overall argument being presented. Use a colour or an asterisk.

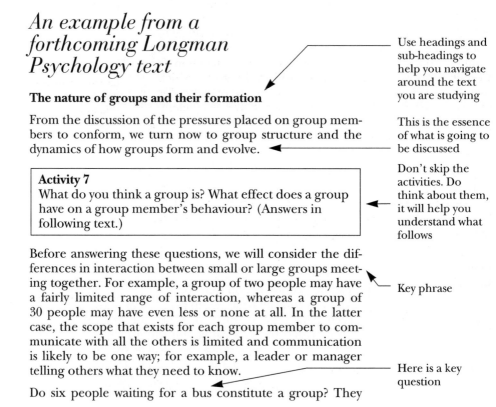

An example from a forthcoming Longman Psychology text

Use headings and sub-headings to help you navigate around the text you are studying

The nature of groups and their formation

From the discussion of the pressures placed on group members to conform, we turn now to group structure and the dynamics of how groups form and evolve.

This is the essence of what is going to be discussed

> **Activity 7**
> What do you think a group is? What effect does a group have on a group member's behaviour? (Answers in following text.)

Don't skip the activities. Do think about them, it will help you understand what follows

Before answering these questions, we will consider the differences in interaction between small or large groups meeting together. For example, a group of two people may have a fairly limited range of interaction, whereas a group of 30 people may have even less or none at all. In the latter case, the scope that exists for each group member to communicate with all the others is limited and communication is likely to be one way; for example, a leader or manager telling others what they need to know.

Key phrase

Do six people waiting for a bus constitute a group? They

Here is a key question

might, but only if the bus is delayed or if something hap- ◄— Here is the answer
pens while they are waiting, to unite them into a group.
Otherwise there will probably be little interaction and they
will remain a collection of individuals.

Bales (1950) suggested that provided each group member ◄— Definition of a
receives some impression of every other member that is   group
sufficiently distinct for them to enable personalised reactions, then a collection of individuals becomes a group.
This implies a group size of not more than 12. _____ Words in bold
                                                            pick out
                                                            important
For groups to form, **interactions** between group members concepts
need to be sustained. If there is a long wait for the bus to
arrive then a group might emerge. There also has to be
some **perception** of the existence of a group and of the ◄— Two key factors
members belonging to it. A prolonged wait for the bus   for groups are
might allow some kind of perceived identity to emerge   given here
amongst the people concerned. Usually, members already
perceive themselves as belonging to a group owing to a
common purpose; for instance, people meeting to plan
action against a proposed library closure.

Members of a group need to adopt **common norms** of   Mark where
behaviour, which may or may not be expressed. Members   longer paragraphs
who disregard the norms lay themselves open to disap-   introduce new
proval, sanctions or even removal from the group. In the point
library example mentioned above, the protesters may provide a roster for a sit-in in the library. The norm would be to
honour this. Any members who failed to take their turn
would be open to disapproval and possibly to sanction.// Look back up this
Certain roles will tend to develop within the group which paragraph to see
members will adopt, either formally or informally; for   how 'affective
example, chair, food preparer or joker. Patterns of liking relations' are
and disliking will emerge among group members. These   defined
are known as **affective relations**. Each relationship will
develop its own set of norms.

A group needs to have shared goals before it forms or
remains a group. These goals may be either internally or
externally set; even in the latter case they will be open to
interpretation and re-interpretation. Additional goals may be
generated in accordance with group norms, as these develop.

There are clearly many kinds of group and it is a pity that so
many reported studies are based on laboratory groups,
brought together only for study purposes. Out of 2,000   Keep your eye
studies reported by McGrath and Altman (1966), only five ◄— open for quotable
percent could be said to be genuinely carried out on natu- statistics
rally formed groups in natural settings.

Don't be shy of writing on your textbook – provided it is yours!
Annotating your text as you work through it is a valuable way of

deepening your grasp of the material you are studying. To illustrate this point we have reproduced one of the paragraphs given above. It shows the sort of annotation you might do whilst reading through.

Members of a group need to adopt **common norms** of be- *Common norms needed*
haviour, <u>which may or may not be expressed</u>. Members
who disregard the norms lay themselves open to disapproval, sanctions or even removal from the group. In the
library example mentioned above, the protesters may provide a roster for a sit-in at the library. The norm would be to
honour this. Any members who failed to take their turn
would be open to disapproval and possibly to sanction.//
Certain roles will <u>tend to develop</u> within the group which
members will adopt, either formally or informally; for
example, chair, food preparer or joker. <u>Patterns of liking</u>
<u>and disliking</u> will emerge among group members. These
are known as **affective relations.** Each relationship will *Affective relations =*
develop its own set of norms. *liking or disliking*

When you have been through the text, making suitable annotations, then you can summarise in notes. If the text is yours, and you have access to it when you revise, then your notes can be quite brief. What follows is an illustration of how you might record the main points given above.

<u>What groups are and how they form</u>

Size is important.
Bales (1950) suggests each member must form impression of all other members. Implies a size of 12.

Formation of groups:
– **interactions** must be sustained
– members must share **perception** of existence of group
– system of **common norms** needed
– **certain roles** tend to develop, e.g., 'Joker'
– **affective relations** (patterns of liking and disliking) emerge
– there is a need for **shared goals**

Study of groups:
– mostly in lab; only **5%** are in natural settings

You will notice that this summary does not contain many illustrations. It has the essential definitions; it has dates and names for important studies (in this case Bales); it has quotable figures. The example of 'Joker' is given, as later you may forget what the writer meant by roles in this context.

If you have to use these notes for the basis of an essay, you will see that they are true to the text but you will have to put them in your own words. By working from notes like this, you can fill them out with your own illustrations, if necessary.

Recording information and ideas

Notes

Once you have completed the analysis of the handout or section of a book or article, you can make notes. Remember, if the text is yours, the notes only have to be brief. You can always refer back to your annotated text. Your work of analysis will mean the main steps of the argument should be clear. Where you will not have access to the book again, then your notes should be fuller.

Your notes should be clear, with sufficient detail, but not overlong. You need to record the essence of an argument and the key points of particular studies or theories. You will often be using the notes for a current essay or for background to practical work. They will also be useful later on, for revision. Make liberal use of headings, sub-headings, underlining and colour. These will make the notes more interesting to read and also more memorable.

Try to ensure that your notes reflect the line of argument set out in the text you are studying. Record the main steps in the argument (these will often be the key points in the paragraphs). Summarise the key illustrative studies (with names and dates given accurately). Differentiate between studies that support a particular argument and those that are critical of it.

Tables

It is often very helpful to use a table to record the main elements of the text you have been studying. With psychology, you are often comparing and contrasting different arguments and theories. A table enables you to summarise this material effectively. Such a table can often allow you to prepare material for an essay as we will see later.

Diagrams

Mind maps

Mind maps are very useful ways of summarising and organising ideas and information. The very act of creating a mind map will help you to understand and to remember what you are studying. In addition, they will enable you to plan for essays. Mind maps also provide an excellent way of pulling together a lot of material for revision purposes (see page 8). The idea of 'mind-mapping' has been developed by Tony Buzan, and your library will probably have one or more of his books. He summarises his ideas, with many illustrations in *The Mind Map Book*, Tony Buzan, BBC Books (1993).

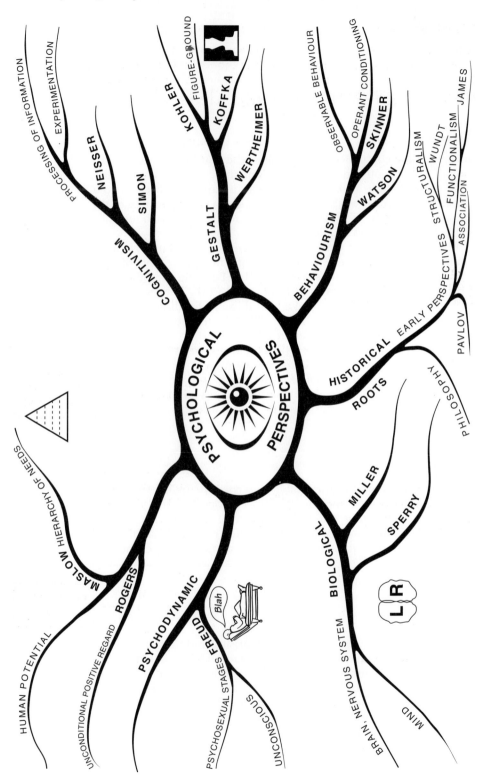

Visual summaries

It is said that 'a picture is worth a thousand words'. If you can summarise an idea with a picture or a diagram, then do so. For example, Freud's ideas on personality structure and the unconscious can be represented in diagrammatic form:

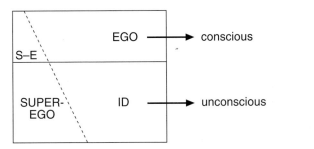

Complex findings can sometimes be represented in a flow chart. There are some interesting examples in Baron and Byrne, *Social Psychology*, Allyn and Bacon (1991).

The drive theory of social facilitation

Presence of others (audience or co-actors) → Heightened arousal → Enhanced tendency to perform dominant

If dominant responses are correct in present condition → Performance is enhanced

If dominant responses are incorrect in present condition → Performance is impaired

Diagram adapted from Baron and Byrne, *Social Psychology* (1991), p. 445

Using information descriptively and analytically

Levels of argument

You will, as part of your course in psychology, be working on two important skills. The first is **comprehending** what other people have written. The second is **re-expressing** those ideas in your own writing. In each case you will find it helpful to understand how arguments are structured. In a way, we are looking at this skill throughout this book, especially in the section on essay writing. We will start by looking at how writers present arguments.

A psychologist, like Eysenck, Freud or Skinner, will use their writing to present a proposition. Freud used his early writings to support the idea that there was such a thing as the *unconscious*. Skinner, in the 1950s, used his writings to establish *behaviourism* as the scientific study of behaviour. Eysenck, who agreed with many ideas in behaviourism, used his writings to establish a *psychometric* approach to some aspects of human behaviour. He was also very critical of Freud.

The propositions presented by psychologists will be supported by specific theories. For example, Skinner developed the theory that behaviour could be understood in terms of *stimulus* and *response*. The theories will be presented and defended in terms of various arguments. The arguments in turn will be supported by specific points that relate to them. Writing in psychology (and other disciplines) can be usefully explored in terms of these different levels. We will look at one way of considering these levels next.

World views

In each case, the famous psychologists we have just mentioned had a broad framework of ideas and assumptions that they presumed was true. Skinner, for example, maintained that psychologists could study only observable behaviour. What could not be directly observed was speculative and non-scientific. In contrast, Freud had at the heart of his model of the human being something that could not be actually measured, namely the unconscious.

This *framework of ideas and assumptions* we will call a **world view** or **perspective.** You will find these assumptions expressed quite clearly by some writers. Others consider their point of view so self-evident that they do not make their assumptions clear. In both comprehending what they are saying and also re-expressing their ideas, you will find it useful to be aware of these perspectives. When you are studying a textbook, it usually is informing you about other people's theories. With each theory, you should try to note what broad model of human nature the proponent of that theory is assuming.

Theories

Psychologists, when they carry out research, are seeking to test whether certain **theories** about behaviour are valid. In their work, they are investigating *propositions*. For example, Craik (1977) has a theory about how we remember things. He believes that the amount of effort that is used in paying attention to something determines whether it is remembered or not. This theory is called 'Levels of Processing'. The notion that the more deeply meaning is encoded, the more likely a word is to be remembered is the proposition that he has tested. Craik's theories about memory fit into the general perspective of cognitive psychology, with its assumptions about the importance of information processing to understand human behaviour. With the psychologists that we study we generally consider the particular theories that they are testing. When we look at writing by, or about, psychologists, then we need to identify these propositions that they are putting forward. We can then begin to assess the next level, namely the argument that they present in support of their proposition.

Arguments

Most of what you will read in your textbooks are **arguments** for or against particular propositions. If you look at the text you are using and consider the part on intelligence, you will probably find a debate on whether intelligence is predominantly inherited, or whether the environment and experience in some way determine intelligence. Both of these are propositions. Both of these propositions rest on broad models or perspectives about the nature of intelligence. For each theoretical position, psychologists have put forward arguments. For example, Burt (1940) suggested that studies of identical twins reared apart indicated that intelligence was mainly inherited. He used the argument that the similarity in intelligence scores of identical twins reared in different environments established that intelligence must be largely innate. A contrasting argument is put in the work of Skeels and Dye (1939). They found that children in an orphanage who were given a more stimulating environment improved their IQ scores by an average of 32 points.

Points

These arguments are generally supported by evidence. With Burt, the evidence was the research he claimed to have carried out on identical twins. With Skeels and Dye, the evidence is their long-term study of children in the orphanage. In looking at arguments, each step, illustration or fact that is put forward to support or to contradict an argument we can call a **point**. Much of what you will read in psychology (and other subjects) are arguments supported by points. The skill in analysis and note taking is to clarify the argument and to record or highlight sufficient of the points to make the argument intelligible.

11

The skill in writing is to be able to reproduce the arguments in your own words; then, in relation to the arguments, to present and assess the points that support them or oppose them.

Further guidance on this skill of working with different levels of an argument is given in *Clear Thinking* by John Inglis and Roger Lewis, National Extension College, Collins (1993). In particular, they show how arguments can also be supported by the use of what they call 'persuader words' and emotive language.

We can summarise the concept of levels of argument with a table:

Levels of argument	Description of level	Illustration: the two-stage theory of memory
Points	Details, descriptions and facts	• Material held in the memory for a short time is coded in terms of what it sounds like (*acoustically*) • Material held in the memory for more than a minute is coded in terms of what it means (*semantically*) • An address presented visually will be encoded acoustically after a few seconds
Arguments	The position or case that the psychologist or writer is trying to establish; using points to support a theory	The short-term memory encodes material in a different form from the long-term memory.
Theories	Propositions and ideas that suggest causes and explanations; in writing, these are supported by arguments	Memory has two different stores, one that is *short term* and one that is *long term*.
World views or perspectives	The fundamental assumptions that underlie particular theories	This approach to memory, based on the work of Atkinson and Shiffrin, assumes the importance of cognitive psychology and *information processing*.

Note taking

Your notes should be clear, with sufficient detail, but not over-long. You need to record the essence of the argument and the key points of particular studies or theories. Some illustrative material to back up arguments is important but don't get lost in detail.

Set out your notes clearly. Even though you will be writing an essay based on them, or introducing a practical, they may still prove valuable for revision later in the course. Make liberal use of headings, subheadings, underlining and colour. These will make your notes clearer and more interesting to read. If you look at the memory section in Psychology textbooks, you will see that use of interesting layout and colour is one way of improving memorability.

Cards

Many students find that writing summaries of studies on cards can prove to be very useful. It is strongly recommended that you do this right from the start of your course. For each main study and theory you should produce a card. This card should have the main points about the study, the author and the date. Material on cards can be easily manipulated when you plan your essay. They will also be invaluable for revision later.

Planning for essays

Essays packed with good material, which one presents haphazardly, will never gain very much credit. Although planning what you are going to write may not be easy, especially early on in the course, it will serve to clarify the ideas that are being written about. The plan should reflect the broad outline of the argument being presented. Before a plan can be made for a given question, the question needs to be analysed. To accomplish this, underline the key words in the question or title. Then try to restate in your own words what the question is saying. Scribble down, in any order, the main points that you wish to include in your answer. These can be worked later into a structured plan. Note whether the question is asking you to 'discuss' or 'explain' or 'evaluate' or 'compare' or 'give evidence', and whether you are expected to 'be critical'.

It may seem like stating the obvious, but a good essay will have a beginning, a middle and an end. There are a number of ways in which you might structure your answer. Here are two:

1 The 'evaluation'
Introduction, with main terms defined
Development of ideas, with illustrations and criticisms
Conclusion in relation to the question set

2 The 'debate'
Introduction, with main issues outlined
One line of argument (with theory and evidence)

The opposing line of argument (with theory and evidence)
Discussion and conclusion

Whereas the overall plan will probably conform to one of these patterns, the detailed structure of the arguments may be more complex. The use of 'thought-webs' or 'mind-maps' can be most helpful in allowing you to build up your plan around certain ideas. This technique is illustrated in the next section. The finished plan for a coursework essay should show where the main arguments and ideas are to be introduced, and what theorists and studies are to be mentioned at various points. Even under examination conditions a brief plan can prove invaluable, and can help ensure that the essay has a good structure.

Planning for practicals

This will be dealt with in detail later on in this text, as there is a format for writing practicals which can be followed quite closely. For the introduction and the discussion sections of the practical, the same ideas about planning apply. It is often necessary to cover a lot of material in relatively few words. This requires you to be clear about what you want to say, and the best order in which to say it. A clear plan will prove invaluable.

Researching the answer – how to use texts

In this next section we will look at two examples of how you might prepare for writing an essay as part of your course. Initially you will have to ensure you understand the question. Then you will need to refer to any relevant notes you have been given and your text books. When preparing an essay, you will find it helpful to organise your information. One way to do this is given below. It involves using a table. The value of this is that you can see the relationship between the various aspects of the question you have researched. It will also be useful later on for revision purposes.

a) **Describe and evaluate one physiological explanation of motivation.**
b) **Describe and evaluate one non-physiological explanation of motivation.**
(AEB 1993)

This is an examination question, with each part carrying almost equal marks. We will look at how you might approach a question like this if it is set as an essay to do in your own time, after research. First you will need to decode the question. You need to find at least one physiological explanation and at least one that is not, whilst still being psychological. You will need to research more than one of each if you are to *evaluate*. An evaluation implies looking at the adequacy of the explanation. This is usefully done comparatively, although each

14

explanation can also be evaluated against its theoretical simplicity, adequacy and the quality of the evidence provided in its support.

You turn to your text. Gross (1992) has a chapter headed 'Motivation, Emotion and Stress'. In the expanded section of contents on page vi, you will find he deals with six related areas: philosophy and psychology of emotion; drive-reduction theory; homeostatic drive theory; competence motives; play and motivation; motivation and adaptation. You will need to select one that is clearly physiological and one that is not. If this is your only text you will have to make the best job of answering the question from this material. Hopefully you will also turn to other sources. Hayes (1994) also has a chapter on 'Motivation and Emotion'. A quick review of pages 421–39 shows drive theories are dealt with in their original form and in their subsequent elaborations. Alternative theories (McClelland, Maslow, Rogers) are then presented. Other texts you may have access to will cover similar ground. If you have dealt with the area in a class, then you should also review your notes.

You choose your two **explanations**. They need to be ones on which there is sufficient information to base a full answer. You may wish to make detailed notes before you start. You should use techniques similar to those suggested earlier in the chapter, *highlighting, dividing, labelling* and *classifying*. Then you will find it helpful to organise the information in a way that relates to the demands of the essay title. A table is helpful.

Explanation	Main concepts	Evidence	Critical points
Drive theory	e.g., What is a drive? Homeostatic drive theory (Cannon) Drive reduction (Hull) etc.	Hunger (Morgan 1943); Cannon and Washburn (1912); Green (1980) Walker (1984) etc.	Rogers (1959) Olds and Milner (1954) Tolman (1948) etc.
McClelland's achievement motivation	Need for achievement etc.		

Under **main concepts,** you would outline the key ideas that relate to each theory. Some examples are given above.

With each point you would briefly mention the **evidence** that relates to that point. This would generally be studies of animals or humans. With the first explanation, the physiological aspects should be considered in some detail. With McClelland, or similar, the aspects that go beyond physiology should be stated.

The final section of **critical points** is where you will record studies, ideas and theories that run counter to the specific points made.

Compare and contrast individual and situational approaches to personality.
(AEB 1994)

In preparing for an answer to this question, it is essential to clarify what in meant by each of the key terms. This question is *not* asking for a comparison of theories based on *types* with theories based on *traits*.

You will find that material on personality is somewhat scattered in some textbooks, because certain theorists (Freud, for example) may be dealt with under various different headings (child development, abnormal behaviour and personality). It is worth making careful use of the index. The *situational approach* may prove the more difficult of the two to locate.

In Gleitman (1991), *Psychology* (third edition, Norton), there are relevant entries in the index under *situationism* and *situational factors*. Looking up 'personality' you will find no mention of situation. With Hayes (1994), however, the only reference to situational demands lands you in the section on intelligence. When you look up personality, you find no direct references to the situational approach. In a position like this, you need to use one text (or your teacher or class notes) to clarify exactly what is meant by the term. Then you need to track down relevant material under other headings.

Gleitman will demonstrate that a key name for the situational approach is Walter Mischel. If you look him up in Hayes, you will then find two pages devoted to his theory; also, the section that deals with Mischel may suggest others who take account of social and situational factors, like Bandura (1977) and Mead (1934). They provide approaches that have some similarity to Mischel, whilst not emphasising the transitory nature of personality to the extent that he does.

The *individual* approach relates to those theories of personality that see it as some sort of fixed and invariant property, either inborn or formed in early childhood. Both type and trait theories would feature here. Those who stress childhood experience for moulding personality, like Freud, might fall under the individual heading *or* that of situationism. They provide a useful focus of discussion.

When you have made notes from your sources it will be helpful to classify your ideas in a way that allows comparisons and contrasts to be drawn. An example of how such a table might begin to look is given below. This is not complete but given by way of illustration.

Approaches	Theories and concepts	Evidence and studies	Critical review
Individual	e.g., Eysenck Neuroticism Extraversion e.g., Studies of 'five robust factors'	Studies of neuroticism Norman (1963); Costa & McCrae (1992)	– Simplistic method of measurement – may overemphasise traits; however, can have practical value
Situational	e.g., Mischel – role of 'personal cognition' – expectancies	He reviewed Hatshorne and May (1928) and then many other studies; found little correlation between tests and actual behaviour	– relates to social learning theory theory (Bandura) – overemphasis on situation now seen as limited
	e.g., Freud – Childhood 'situation' forms personality e.g., Fromm – Exploitative characters, etc.	– Studies of oral, anal and phallic 'types' – 'Little Hans' fear, and Oedipus complex – Historical review of role of society	– evidence limited for Freud – Fromm has developed Freud's ideas

Planning the answer – how to use arguments

This idea of using tables can be elaborated as you become more familiar with the subject matter. Once you have begun to get a grasp of the different schools of psychology, how they relate and what their basic assumptions are, you can use this knowledge to organise your answer. In the two examples given below the tables are based around different *levels* of argument. This concept of levels of argument has been discussed already on page 10.

Describe and discuss how sensory processes relate to perception.
(AEB 1991)

The question uses two technical terms: *sensory processes* and *perception*. If you are not clear what is meant by these terms then you will need to find out. This will be essential if you are to establish the boundaries of your answer. Neither Gross (1992) nor Hayes (1994) in their A-level texts mention 'sensory processes' in their indexes. However, if you look at the list of contents in Gross you will find that the whole of Part Three is referring to sensory and cognitive processes. His Chapter 8 is headed 'Sensory Processes'. This – as the table of contents shows – deals with sensory systems (visual and auditory). The next chapter deals with 'Perception'.

Hayes does not provide an annotated list of contents. The relevant parts of her Chapter 2 appear to be 'Perceptual Organisation' and 'Explaining Perception'.

Sensory processes could refer to any of the senses. You will probably want to focus on vision. Hearing will also be relevant. You are being asked in the question to look at the *relationship* between sensory processes and perception. How does one lead to the other; what are the connections; in what way are they different? You could organise your notes into a table, before embarking on the essay.

Aspects of the answer	Points	Arguments	Theories	World views
Sensory processes	• sense organs (e.g., eye and ear) • sense receptors (e.g., rods and cones) connection with brain area • auditory sensory processing	• is the eye a camera? • colour vision	• trichromatic theory • opponent colour theory	• perception is fundamentally about physical processes that can be measured
Perception	• figure-ground • depth perception • pattern recognition	• needs sensation • bottom up (driven by data) • top down (role of perceptual set) • illusions (top down explanations)	• pandemonium model (bottom up • Marr's computational theory (bottom up) Gregory	• innate (inborn) vs. environmental (Lockian approach)
Connection between the two	• sensory information is processed	• what is 'seen' and 'heard' goes beyond the basic sensations	• Neisser – combination of top down and bottom up	• human perception is an active constructive process

All the ideas in this table come from either Gross (1992) or Hayes (1994)

The effort to classify the information you are going to use in the essay will help you to understand the ideas better. Working from a table such as this one, you will be able to plan an effective answer; all the material is in front of you. The table will also be useful later on, when you come to revise.

Describe the main features of the scientific method and assess the appropriateness of this method to the study of human behaviour.
(AEB 1994)

This question falls obviously into two parts. The first is concerned with a *description* of the scientific method. The second is an *assessment* of how appropriate the method is for the study of *human behaviour*. We should note the question emphasises *human behaviour*. This question is not asking whether psychology is scientific, nor does it require a detailed analysis of the *experimental* method.

The answer to the first part of the question should be structured in such a way that it can be used to address the second part of the question. You can decide whether to deal with the descriptive parts prior to the assessment, when you have a clearer overview of what you wish to deal with. It will be helpful to consider the answer in terms of levels of argument.

Aspects of the answer	Points	Arguments	Theories	World views
The scientific method	• e.g., use of experimentation inductive control groups, measurement	• what is meant by 'objective'? • what is meant by 'empirical'? • what is meant by 'control'? • what is meant by the testing of hypotheses?	1 classical view of science 2 Popper's approach	1 objective world 'out there' can be discovered inductively 2 theories determine questions (hypotheses) asked (Popper)
Objectivity	• science claims be objective • value freedom • control • replicability	• the scientific method is designed for objectivity • some psychology can be objective in the same way – by using the scientific method(s) • some psychology cannot be approached in quite the same way	1 behaviourism aims to be objective and empirical 2 developmental psychology and and social psychology deal with self-conscious subjects 3 psychodynamic psychology cannot fit the purely scientific model	1 behaviourism: the only good psychology is 'objective' 2 the subject matter of psychology different from that of the natural sciences 3 the subjective and the unconscious have a valid place in psychology

Aspects of the answer	Points	Arguments	Theories	World views
Domains of psychology	• cognitive: memory, perception, thinking • social: groups; leadership • personality: Eysenck; Maslow; Freud; e.g., Maslow's literary approach; Freud's case-study approach	1 cognitive: often uses lab type 2 social uses experiments but less objective 3 areas of personality research are quite subjective	1 psychology is a science like any other 2 psychology needs to adapt to its special subject matter 3 self-actualisation, Oedipus complex, go beyond normal scientific investigation	1 behaviourist and cognitive view of psychology as 'science of behaviour' 2 'real' occurs in natural setting 3 psychology legitimately goes beyond the method of the natural sciences
Observation	• taking readings in physics or chemistry • contrast scientist and newspaper reporter • the 'uncertainty principle' in physics • Festinger *When Prophecy Fails* (1958)	• scientific observation is always objective • non-objective observation is useless • observation in psychology cannot always be objective • need for participant observation	1 Newtonian science 2 quantum physics (e.g. Heisenberg) 3 participant observation enables 'insight'	1 the observer in science is separate from the observation 2 the observer always influences the thing observed 3 'insight' is a valid form of knowledge

Working from a table like this, you can develop your answer by dealing with the more descriptive first section (the scientific method). Then you can take up the arguments that enable you to assess the appropriateness of this method. These can be related to specific illustrative **points**, and also to the **theories** and **viewpoints** that underpin them.

Writing psychology essays

Both the examination essay and essays done as part of your course are used to test your ability to describe and analyse psychological theories and the findings that support or refute them; to make comparisons of theories; to select and weigh evidence in support of an argument; and to express critical judgements.

Lack of success at A-level often comes from the result of either:

a) writing at a level appropriate for GCSE, that is factually based, but not bridging the gap to A-level work, which requires a greater emphasis on the relationship between theory and actual research;

or

b) the all-and-sundry answer that combines assertions, common sense, with nuggets of psychological research, not effectively related to the question.

The highest grades are achieved by those who are able to amass a considerable amount of information relating to a topic, in an orderly and coherent way. Such essays exhibit a clear line of argument, with each part related to the one before and the one that follows. The essay rests on a sound factual basis and also develops and discusses the appropriate concepts and theories.

Often a major weakness of essays done at home, or under test conditions, is irrelevance. You must answer the question that is set. Make a plan. When the plan is complete then check that it does actually answer the question. In a woodwork room in a school there was a sign on the wall – 'Think twice, cut once'. The same principle applies to essay writing. Checking your plan against the question means that you will not go off at a tangent. When actually writing, check frequently that the points you are making and the arguments you are developing are clearly linked to the main issues in the question.

The essay

The purpose of this type of work, which is usually done at home, is to enable you to present, in your own words, the ideas and arguments relating to a particular issue or question. Generally such an essay is set after you have gone over the issue in class. It is a chance for you to re-express the ideas that have been presented to you. By so doing you have the opportunity really to grasp the significance of what you have been taught, and to move from knowledge about a topic, largely contained in your notes, to understanding. A topic, when really understood, is much easier to remember. Consequently, you can see an essay, if worked on effectively, can be of real value in preparing you for the examination (and, incidentally, helping you to grasp some of the main issues in psychology for their own sake). The ability to present complex arguments is a valuable skill in itself. Writing essays can help you to develop this communication skill if you keep in mind certain principles:

1 You should prepare for the essay adequately. Don't let it be a 'last minute job', accomplished amid the detritus of a coffee bar, on the morning that it is due! Equally, the best essays are not those written with one eye on the TV.

2 Make a detailed plan. Know where you are going to put the various arguments before you start. The plan gives you an overview of what you are going to write at various stages. This means that each section is a coherent part of the whole.

3 Make your opening relevant. You should commence with an issue, idea or finding that is of particular relevance to the question that you are tackling. This should indicate the angle or direction that you will follow.

4 Link the main stages of your argument. Give signposts that the reader can follow.

5 Imagine that you are writing for an intelligent person, who is well read but not familiar with this topic. In other words give sufficient detail, without having to go into all the minutiae.

6 Generally allow each idea or study a paragraph of its own. Then link the paragraphs together, so that the argument flows.

7 Finally, make sure that, as you approach the end, you round off what you are saying. Establish a conclusion, or at least sum up what you see as being the balance of the arguments that you have presented. The conclusion allows you to review critically the relative merits of the various arguments in the essay.

The coursework essay should be comprehensive in its coverage of a topic. This will help both in understanding the issues and also as a revision aid later. You need therefore to be accurate in the details that you quote. Make an effort to explain and discuss the theories and ideas that you present. Often the essay will be the final piece of work you do on a topic before you prepare for the examination. So it is when you write the essay that you should invest the time and effort to ensure that you really understand what you are writing about.

The examination essay

The purpose of the examination essay is to test your knowledge of psychology, your understanding of the theories and your ability to give clear expression to your ideas. Your purpose in writing the essay is to score high marks. This you will do by showing that you really comprehend the question and then providing a well-organised and informed answer. This whole book is designed to help you accomplish this, but here are some pointers that can help.

Always read the question through at least twice to ensure that you really understand what is actually being asked. The folly of answering a question that has not been set is obvious, and results in much wasted effort and heartache. Then go through the question again and underline the key terms. This will ensure that you will not miss any vital points. Then make a plan. This will not be elaborate, as under examination conditions you will not have the time. But it should be adequate. It is surprising how much you can get down on paper in two or three minutes, and it is time very well spent. When completed, check your plan against the question to ensure that you have answered what has actually been set.

There are three elements to bear in mind when writing an examination essay: structure, content and style. The *structure* of the essay refers to the way in which you organise the argument. It should be logical, clear and appropriate. Your argument should unfold through linked paragraphs, and the main sections of the essay should form a coherent whole. The *content* refers to the substance of the essay. This must be appropriate and in sufficient detail. It relates to the level of conceptual development in the essay. In other words, how far the main concepts implicit in the arguments are explained and developed. Also, it is concerned with the ability to set what you write in a theoretical context. The *style* is your own way of expressing ideas. The essay should be as clear as possible, but there is room for a little ingenuity and originality in the presentation.

In the next section we will start by looking in detail at how an essay is planned and written.

Constructing an essay
Outline and evaluate one theory of cognitive development

Analysis of the question

The first step in tackling the question is to consider the key words and phrases. These can be underlined for greater clarity.
<u>Outline</u> and <u>evaluate</u> the <u>one theory</u> of <u>cognitive development</u>
The question can now be analysed in more detail. You need to decide which theory to use: Piaget is appropriate.

<u>Outline</u>   this implies giving an overview picking out the main points of Piaget's theories and experiments.

<u>Evaluate</u>   this prompts us to consider the value of Piaget's work. What is of lasting significance? What aspects have been criticised? What is the status of his work?

<u>Cognitive development</u>   this gives us the subject matter. This is the intellectual development of the child as investigated by Piaget.

<u>Child development</u>   this gives us our subject matter – namely all that is encompassed by the term 'child development'.

Planning the question

When preparing an essay for class, a plan is valuable. It provides a checklist to make sure that what you are going to cover is adequate, and most important, will answer the question. A brief plan is very helpful even when writing under examination conditions.

As a start a list of points could be made. Initially, write them down as they occur. They can be organised later. At this stage go for completeness.

Piaget's theory	*Empirical studies*	*Critical points*
Biologist	Object permanence	Bower
Evolutionary theory	Conservation	Donaldson
Cognitive development	Mountain experiment	Hughes
	Beaker problem	Gelman and Gallistel
Four main stages	Play	'Naughty Teddy'
Moral development	Rules and morals	Language use
Egocentrism		Bruner
His methodology		
Assimilation		
Schemas		

This initial list may be added to as you continue your planning. However, the purpose of an essay is not to put down everything you know or can find out about a topic, rather it is to answer effectively the question drawing on relevant information to support your argument. You are now in a position to move on to a plan for the essay. This can be in the form of a mind-map or thought-web, or a sequential list. We will illustrate both here. In exam conditions only a brief version of these will be possible.

The plan should pick out the fundamental structure of the argument that you wish to make. If this is clear to you, then your essay will gain in coherence and relevance.

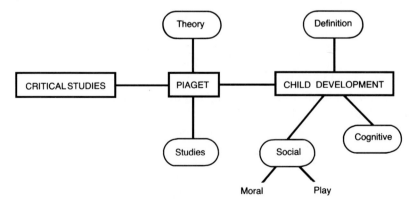

This initial plan indicates the three aspects of the answer, namely:

1 what is child development

2 what is Piaget's contribution to our understanding of it, and

3 what critical evaluation has been made of Piaget's work?

A fuller plan would look like this:

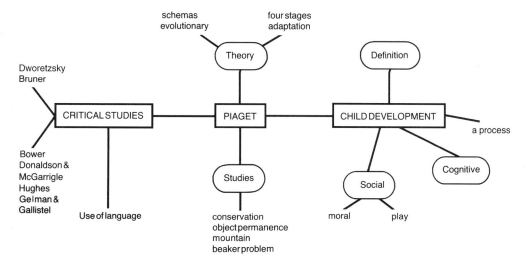

The value of a map like this is that the whole argument can be seen at a glance, and the relationship between parts of the argument made apparent. However, it is also quite acceptable to do a straightforward linear plan. Use whichever method you find suits you best.

Child development
    Definition
    Cognitive development – a process
    Social development – moral; play

Piaget
    His theory
    – biological basis; evolutionary
    – schemas
    – adaptation
    – four stages

Studies
    – observation
    – object permanence
    – conservation experiments
    – mountain – egocentrism
    – beaker problem – formal

Critical studies
    – Bower – object permanence
    – Donaldson and McGarrigle – Naughty teddy
    – Hughes – police doll and boy doll
    – Gelman and Gallistel – number
    – use of language

    – Dworetzsky
    – Bruner

Concluding evaluation

What follows is one possible answer to this question. This is the only 'model answer' in the book and it should be understood that there would be many other ways to deal with this question just as adequately.

As will be the practice later in the book, a brief commentary is provided to explain why the question is being approached in this way. The length of the essay is what could be achieved by most A-level students under exam conditions.

Piaget, a Swiss biologist, turned his attention to cognitive development in children, after working with Binet on the development of IQ tests. While his primary interest was cognitive development, he considered other aspects of child development including moral development and the role of play. **(1)** The term development implies two aspects. The first is a maturational component, with a biological basis. The second is a learned component. Piaget was concerned with the interaction between these two aspects. He investigated the process of the development of intelligence and moral thought. **(2)**

There are four basic stages in the Piagetian approach to child development. These are the sensorimotor stage (0–2 years); the pre-operational stage (2–7 years); the concrete operational stage (7–11 years); and finally the formal operational stage (11 years and over). These stages are discontinuous in the sense that they mark quite distinctly different ways of representing and understanding the world. **(3)** Piaget was intrigued by how the child made sense of the world. He explained this in terms of schemas, or internal representations, and the process of adaptation. Adaptation consists of two complementary activities. Assimilation, which is where experience of the environment is absorbed into already existing schemas, and accommodation, where new experience leads to disequilibrium and can only be dealt with by a change in schemas. **(4)**

Piaget's theory is based on extensive observational studies, which he carried out with children. It is this firm foundation of empirical support that has made his work so influential, even if some of the details of his findings have been criticised. **(5)**

In the first four months of the sensorimotor stage the child has no sense of object permanence. It is a case of 'out of sight and out a mind'. Bower (1972), however, disputes this and showed that, with the right experimental technique, a child will

(1) The introduction is directly related to the question and lays the groundwork for explaining what 'Piagetian' means as well as picking out what will be covered later.

(2) The first part of the plan has now been dealt with, albeit in a very succinct manner.

(3) The temptation here is to write at length on the stages. However, only as much detail as is necessary for the question need be given.

(4) Again, a degree of Piaget's 'pure theory' needs to be covered, but can be dealt with briefly.

(5) It is important to mention Piaget's methodology.

track an object and show surprise if it does not re-appear after passing behind a screen. **(6)**

Many of Piaget's experiments were concerned with conservation – of mass, of volume and of number. He demonstrated that in the pre-operational stage a child will perceive liquid poured from a short, fat glass to a long thin one, as having increased. The child conceives that there is 'more' liquid in the thinner glass. In other words he/she cannot conserve volume. Similar findings were established with regard to mass (using Plasticine) and number (using coins or counters). Children up to the age of 7 tended to see change of shape or form as indicating some substantial change. **(7)**

While the basic premise, that children do not have a clear schema for conservation at this age, is broadly accepted, there have been critical studies. Donaldson and McGarrigle (1979) used a 'Naughty Teddy' to make the re-arrangements. They found the child would show conservation much younger with the Naughty Teddy than with the experimenter. Using sugar mice, and simple sleight-of-hand, Gelman and Gallistel (1978) showed that children had much more sense of number than Piaget had given them credit for, even if they could not count in the accepted adult way. Donaldson (1970) suggested that the very language used in these experiments could confuse the children. **(8)** During this period a notable feature of the child's thought is egocentrism, which will be considered next.

The child, says Piaget, is egocentric and tends to see things from his/her own standpoint. This he demonstrated with the classic mountain view experiment. He showed that pre-operational children tended to assume that a doll, looking at a model mountain scene, would see the same view that they did. Subsequent studies, notably that of Hughes (1984) using an interesting cross of walls, suggested otherwise. In Hughes' study children had to hide a 'boy-doll' from 'policemen dolls'. He showed that $3\frac{1}{2}$ to 5 year olds were successful, in working out the policeman's viewpoint, 90% of the time. **(9)**

In the next stage, of concrete operations, Piaget demonstrated that the child becomes able to classify to a much greater extent. However, certain logic problems can only be solved with physical objects and cannot be worked out mentally until about the age of 11.

At 11 the child begins to achieve formal operations. They can now manipulate ideas, and approach scientific problems in a logical way. This Piaget demonstrated with a simple experiment involving working out how to mix various combinations of colourless liquids. The child who has achieved formal operations will not be random in his/her procedure.

Work by Dworetzsky (1981) has supported Piaget's,

(6) Again, this is a very brief summary, both of Piaget's ideas and that of Bower. The choice has been made here to make contrasts as the essay unfolds, rather than deal first with Piaget and then with his critics. Either approach will do.

(7) It is possible to give brief sketches to illustrate these experiments, but only where they will save time in writing.

(8) At this point the section on conversation is completed as far as time and space allows. A link needs to be made to the next idea, which is egocentrism.

(9) Exam essays do not need to be packed with facts and figures, but some should be learned. Also roughly when people did their studies should be remembered.

showing that the adolescent can think hypothetically. Other studies – (notably Wason (1965) and Dulitt (1972) – have shown many adults never appear to achieve this stage.

While Piaget's main focus has been cognitive development, he has applied his ideas in other areas as well. **(10)** He suggests the child goes through distinct stages of moral development, which link to their understanding of rules. The moral judgement of the child changes as they come to be able to understand intention. Piaget tested this idea using hypothetical stories. His work has been extended by Kohlberg, who developed a more elaborate theory of six stages.

(10) Here again is an explicit link, so the essay does not jump from point to point.

Piaget has shown that children's play goes through similar stages. Overall, his theory appears to hold together well. It has formed the basis of other theoretical developments – like that of Bruner and Kohlberg. It also has been very influential on the profession of teaching, especially in the structuring of activities in the primary school. **(11)**

While other theorists like Freud and Skinner have raised very different issues to those of Piaget, his work on cognitive development stands up well to his critics.

(11) The essay need not end with a summary, but rather should conclude in relation to the actual question.

Questions in parts

A particular type of question that you may come across will be in several parts. We have already seen one example of this when we looked at 'Researching the answer ...' on page 14. When a question is in parts it is important to see what each part requires and to separate your response clearly into the correct parts. Consider the following:

Outline the main features of Social Learning Theory. (*5 marks*)
(AEB 1995)

This is one part of a two-part question. The second part carries 20 marks. Under examination conditions, where you would have about 45 minutes to answer this question, this first part would be worth one fifth of that time, or about 8 to 9 minutes. A common mistake that is made in tackling questions like this is either to give such a brief response that it earns only one or two marks, or to write so much that insufficient time and space is left for the second and more substantial part of the question. When only 5 marks are on offer, then the answer is very likely to be entirely descriptive and not to involve evaluation or analysis.

A clear definition of Social Learning Theory is asked for. Its historical origins in the 1940s, as an offshoot of behaviourism, through the work of Dollard and Miller, might be mentioned. More recent work of Bandura and also of Mischel, provides the main concepts. No evaluation or comparison is asked for. None should be given. The second part of the question allows for a critical approach.

Critically consider the contribution of Social Learning Theory to an understanding of the development of *either* gender roles *or* social motives (such as achievement, approval, affiliation). (*20 marks*)

Under test conditions you would have about 35 minutes to tackle this second part. You would need to choose which of the two areas to concentrate on: gender or social motives. Having made your choice you will need to consider the strengths of the Social Learning approach in dealing with that field, and also its limitations. Let us assume you choose gender roles.

You will have to explain clearly what is meant by gender roles. Having established what gender roles are, the rest of the answer should consider how effectively Social Learning Theory explains their development. A description of the contribution of the theory has to be part of the answer. What is being sought is the adequacy of the theory. First, how much does it explain? Are there aspects of gender roles it does not deal with? How useful is the concept of *imitation?* What is the role of the media? How do they explain the impact of child-rearing practices? Second, what is the evidence to back up the theory? You need to give named studies. Third, are other theories better able to deal with aspects of gender development? These would need to be mentioned briefly; for example, the behaviourist approach and that of psychoanalysis. The cognitive work of Kohlberg might also be considered. In each case they should be related to and contrasted with the fundamental assumptions of Social Learning Theory.

a) Describe psychological explanations of forgetting. (*10 marks*)
b) Discuss practical applications which have developed from such explanations. (*15 marks*)
(AEB 1994)

Under test conditions the division of time will be more even than in the previous example, but should relate to the number of marks on offer. In this case the first part should receive 15 to 18 minutes and the second about 25 to 30. The two parts of the question are asking for different skills to be demonstrated. It is important to make sure the emphasis in the first part is on *description* and in the second part, on *discussion.* A careful plan – even under the pressures of exam conditions – will ensure that you do not cover parts in one section that ought to be in the other. You will almost certainly lose marks if you do.

You are asked in the first part to describe explanations of forgetting. Note that you are expected to provide descriptions of the main explanations. These could include: limitations of the short-term memory (Miller) and serial position (Glanzer); interference theory; decay theory; reconstruction theory (Loftus); motivation theory, repression and amnesia (Freud; MacLean); role of context and cues (Baddeley).

With each explanation you provide, there are implications for practical applications. These could be picked up in the second section. Here a *discussion* is called for. This means that each application should be looked at from varying points of view. It goes beyond mere description.

Explanation	Discussion points
Short-term memory	• Use of chunking • Short words more easily retained • Relation to reading comprehension (Daneman & Carpenter 1980) • Use of primacy effect

Interference theory
Decay theory
	• Use of study habits and mnemonic devices to *avoid* these effects:
	  • pegwords
	  • links
	  • method of loci

Reconstruction theory	• Eyewitness testimony (Loftus 1974) • Children as eyewitnesses (Ceci and Brock 1993) • Reinstatement of the context (Krafta & Penrod 1985)
Repression and amnesia	• False memory syndrome
Context and cues	• Divers and learning (Baddeley 1975) • Mood-dependent memory (Bower 1981)

Examples are drawn from Atkinson *et al.* (1993) *Introduction to Psychology*, HBJ and from Sdorow (1995) *Psychology*, Brown and Benchmark

The discussion will be in terms of either the issue of accuracy of memory, or the question of avoiding forgetting. The areas of eyewitness testimony, false memory syndrome and context and cues, provide a rich area for exploring varying viewpoints. The others could be mentioned more in passing.

Preparing an answer – using mind maps

We have looked at a number of ways in which you can record information in a way that will help you in writing analytical and discursive essays. The use of tables is a clear and effective method. The use of mind maps can also represent the subtle way in which thoughts are connected. We have already briefly considered the technique on page 7. Here are two more examples.

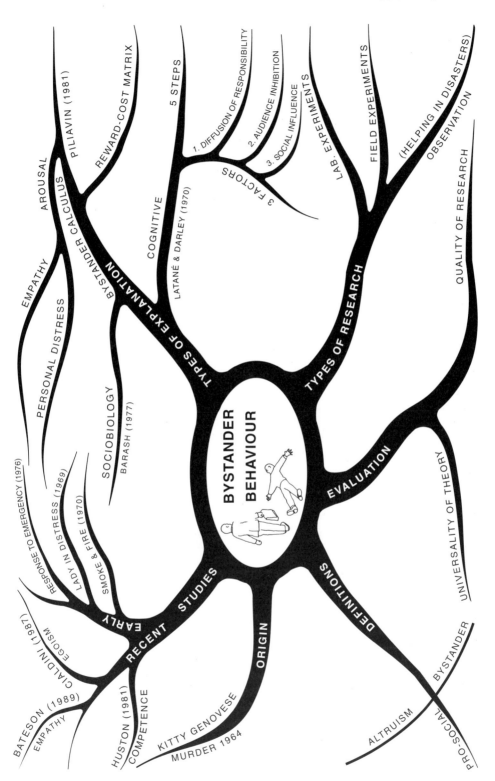

Central node: **BYSTANDER BEHAVIOUR**

TYPES OF EXPLANATION
- BYSTANDER CALCULUS
  - PILIAVIN (1981)
  - REWARD-COST MATRIX
  - AROUSAL
    - EMPATHY
  - PERSONAL DISTRESS
- COGNITIVE
  - LATANÉ & DARLEY (1970)
  - 5 STEPS
  - 3 FACTORS
    - 1. DIFFUSION OF RESPONSIBILITY
    - 2. AUDIENCE INHIBITION
    - 3. SOCIAL INFLUENCE
- SOCIOBIOLOGY
  - BARASH (1977)

TYPES OF RESEARCH
- LAB. EXPERIMENTS
- FIELD EXPERIMENTS
- OBSERVATION
  - (HELPING IN DISASTERS)
- QUALITY OF RESEARCH

EVALUATION
- UNIVERSALITY OF THEORY

DEFINITIONS
- BYSTANDER
- PRO-SOCIAL
- ALTRUISM

ORIGIN
- KITTY GENOVESE
- MURDER 1964

RECENT STUDIES
- HUSTON (1981)
  - COMPETENCE

EARLY STUDIES
- RESPONSE TO EMERGENCY (1976)
- LADY IN DISTRESS (1969)
- SMOKE & FIRE (1970)
- CIALDINI (1987)
  - EGOISM
- BATESON (1989)
  - EMPATHY

31

Describe and evaluate research into bystander behaviour.
(AEB 1995)

Your mind-map should develop both aspects of the question; a description of what bystander behaviour is and who has studied it, and an evaluation of the research and the theory. In preparing for an essay on this topic, review the texts and your notes in the ways already described earlier in this book. When you are confident that you have some understanding, then start your mind-map. Remember to develop it from central ideas to those that are more a question of detail. (See Bystander Behaviour mind-map, page 31).

When your mind-map is complete, you will be in a better position to decide how to express the range of ideas in the essay. It is all in front of you, on the 'map'. You can decide in what order to deal with the ideas whilst being aware of how they relate to one another.

Critically consider the view that the self *develops* as a result of the socialisation process.
(AEB 1993)

As the operative word here is *critically*, the mind-map should develop the various criticisms of the view of the self as *developmental*. The terms *self, development* and *socialisation* should feature on the map. (See Self mind-map, page 33).

A critical review does not mean one that just finds fault. Rather, it is a careful assessment of the evidence for a viewpoint, and its strengths as well as its weaknesses.

How far is the origin of the self explained by the concept of socialisation? Are there aspects of the self that are not a result of the socialisation process? Clearly, you must define carefully what is meant by socialisation. Then you should look at the main theories of self development, to see how far the concept of socialisation is relevant.

Discuss some of the criticisms that have been made of any ONE therapeutic approach.

Although one approach must be chosen, criticisms will often come implicitly or explicitly from others. The criticisms will generally address:

1 theoretical assumptions,

2 clinical practice,

3 success rates.

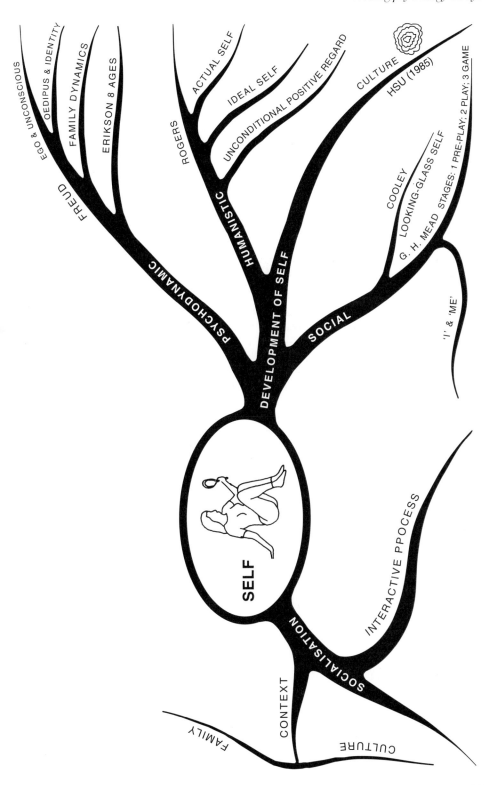

A clear, but brief, presentation of the approach is necessary, indicating its theoretical basis and the techniques used. Alternatives within the particular approach (e.g., psychoanalysis and client-centred therapy, or cognitive therapy and personal construct therapy) could be brought out. Then the criticisms should be considered and backed with evidence.

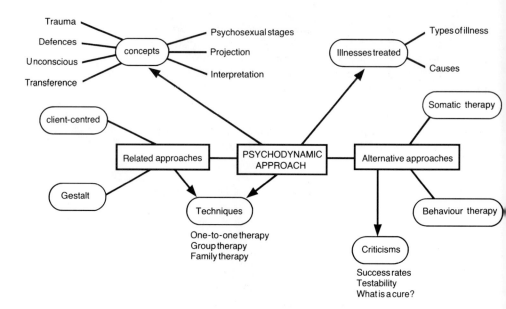

Using psychodynamic therapy as an example, the Freudian assumptions should be outlined. The differences with, say, Jung and Erikson, could be mentioned. Related approaches would include both Carl Rogers' client-centred therapy, and Fritz Perls' work with Gestalt. All use similar techniques. The key concepts underlying the psychodynamic approach (especially trauma, repression and transference) should be looked at critically. They could be contrasted with the system related approach of behavioural therapy. The issue of scientificity could be considered. The methods of treatment – such as 'talking therapies', could be contrasted with the behavioural modification techniques and drug therapies. Much of this question revolves around what constitutes a 'cure'. The problem of defining mental illness and the relevance of the different approaches to neuroses, psychoses and personality disorders is raised in consequence. The claim by Eysenck that psychoanalysis has a lower success rate (44%) than 'spontaneous remission' (66%) is countered by Bergin's more thorough survey (1971) and that of Smith (1980), who argue for a significant improvement in over 80% of the patients.

Examples of essays written under test conditions

In this next section we will look at specific examples of essays written in 45 minutes, under test conditions. They show what can be achieved for an examination. They are not all equally good, although they are all very competent answers. It is worth repeating that this whole book is showing possible ways of approaching psychology questions and practicals. These ways are *not* the only ways.

Discuss the assumptions of the medical approach to the concepts of normal and abnormal behaviour.
(AEB 1990)

The influence of the medical model began at a time **(1)** when the medical profession had begun to find many cures for physical diseases and doctors were hailed as miracle workers. The influence of the church in earlier years had started to fade and so people were looking elsewhere for answers. The church's theory of abnormality was that the person was in contact with evil spirits or had been possessed and so many innocent or mentally ill people were killed or exorcised in ceremonies performed by religious persons. Johann Weyer **(2)** had written a book concerning mental illness and abnormal behaviour claiming it could be treated in other ways. As the church began to lose its grip on society, people began to take note of Johann Weyer's words. Institutions were opened for the mentally ill. Treatment for these people was barbaric and without feeling. Many were treated like animals and chained to the walls.

Pinel **(3)** introduced the humanistic approach and said that mental illness originated from lack of space and inability to cope with the outside world and so patients should be treated as people and with care. Orderlies became care assistants and chains were unlocked. Pinel's humanistic approach enjoyed a short reign but left a very effective mark on the treatment of mental illnesses. As the medical world began to flourish and physical illnesses were cured, many doctors and members of the public began to think that there must be a link between mental and physical illness. Mental illness can be treated **(4)** like physical illness and has an organic origin so all abnormal behaviour can be cured by drugs and by adjusting the brain or the body. Social and personal factors

(1) It is appropriate to start historically, but broad dates would help.

(2) Weyer wrote in the sixteenth century. It is important to place him in a context.

(3) Again, a date is needed (1780s).

(4) Change of tense is inappropriate. The writer is now dealing with *medical assumptions* – this should be emphasised more.

35

weren't taken into consideration. Kraepelin (1913) invented the first diagnostic system. All abnormal behaviour fits into two categories, psychoses and neuroses. Psychoses – not in touch with reality; and neuroses – too much in touch with reality. **(5)** This was heavily criticised and found to be very inaccurate when identifying abnormal behaviour, as shown by a classic study by Rosenham. **(6)** Eight normal people went for a psychiatric evaluation, all complaining of just one symptom – hearing voices. Seven out of the eight were diagnosed as having schizophrenia and admitted. Once admitted, the subjects all began to behave normally but it took between 7 and 52 days for them all to be discharged. Even then they were diagnosed as having schizophrenia, but in remission. **(7)**

Thomas Szasz **(8)** is a very strong critic of the medical model. He says that mental illness is a myth and that the only reason why the medical model was so widely accepted was because it justified taking people out of society, into care, to prevent embarrassment to family and friends. It reduced the discomfort of the surrounding people and the person being labelled sick was happy to be labelled sick, as it shifted the responsibility for their actions. The medical profession was very persuasive.

The medical model's approach to abnormality suggests many things as being true although they are absurd. A person may be eccentric but is labelled abnormal as it makes the people in the surroundings feel uncomfortable (audience effect). So if a person doesn't conform to society's expectations they are immediately thought of as having a mental illness. This leads to social determinism and politically correct behaviour (Allman and Jaffe). Psychiatrists often make their value judgements according to their social class. If the person does not fit in they are labelled mentally ill. What may be abnormal in one part of the world may be normal in another. So hearing voices in East Africa may be due to norms, beliefs and values but in England hearing voices would be a sign of someone being disturbed. The person would be asked to seek a psychiatric evaluation. The deviation from the norm, similar to the statistical approach, states that the whole population fits into the normal curve of distribution. A large percentage are in the middle and very few at either extreme. If this was so for IQ, then people with high and low IQ would be seen as being abnormal. Abnormality is also seen as not coping with everyday life. Normality is seen as coping. Everyone goes through stress, anxiety and depression at some time in life, so when do the levels of these surpass the acceptable

(5) Interesting brief definitions.

(6) We have jumped to the 1970s. This should be acknowledged.

(7) This is a good brief summary of Rosenham's famous study.

(8) We have now moved on to criticisms of the medical model. The assumptions of this model have not yet been fully presented.

levels and a person is seen as having a mental illness. Normality is a lot more difficult to define than abnormality. **(9)**

Due to the problems in Kraepelin's definition, a new diagnostic system was introduced; the DSM III and the DSM III revised (1980–1987). This is the diagnostic system manual for mental illnesses. Instead of labelling all illnesses under only two headings many social factors are included, e.g., psychological disorders, physical disorders, general mental disorders, social factors and how the person has coped over the last year. Szasz has also criticised this as he says that social criteria are used to describe mental illnesses. **(10)** Szasz says it should be defined as a problem of living. Abnormality does not seem to have an organic origin but the medical model believes so and uses chemical, electrical and physical treatments in adjusting the way the brain and body works and accordingly all symptoms should disappear, which just is not so.

Samantha Harding

(9) This paragraph tackles the issue of normality quite well, linking it to the medical approach.

(10) Here the medical classification is mentioned and then linked usefully to a criticism.

This is an interesting response because it is wide ranging. The *content* is quite extensive, and in places considerable ground is covered succinctly. A clearer statement of the fundamental assumptions of the medical model would help. The attempt to see the medical model in an historical context is useful and relevant. Important dates must be given and sometimes they were not. It is the time sequence which has provided the main *structure* of the answer. This could be made explicit at the beginning. There is a fairly successful attempt at both analysis and evaluation, presenting a series of criticisms of the medical model. Some further criticisms (e.g., Heather; Bailey) could be given. The *style* of the answer is appropriate; apart from some inconsistency in using tenses, the points are made clearly.

What is the relationship between language and thought?

There are two theories put forward as to the relationship between thought and language: that of Piaget and Vygotsky who see thought as the primary function, and the Whorf-Sapir linguistic relativity theory where language is seen as the primary function. **(1)** Whorf-Sapir put forward a strong form: language determines thought; and a weak form: language can influence thought. There is no evidence to support the strong form but there is evidence for the weak form of their theory. **(2)**

Piaget says language is a tool which facilitates the thinking process and this would appear to hold true. Several studies

(1) The essay commences in a way that is immediately relevant to the issue of the nature of the relationship between language and thought.

(2) This paragraph serves as a pointer for issues that are tackled more fully later in the essay.

37

have shown that thought goes on without language being readily available. Object permanence can be seen as the first sign of symbolic thought in a child at a time when it is unable to speak. In fact, when a child does learn to talk, it first utters one- and two-word messages which convey a greater meaning than the words uttered. **(3)** This is evidence for a complex thinking process going on in the child's head. Telegraphic speech is the best example of information being organised into a minimal amount to convey maximum information. Evidence for thought without the need for language is shown by Firth (1966), who reports that deaf and mute non-signing adults score equally with 'normal' adults on IQ tests. This links to Bernstein's restricted and elaborated codes where working-class children who use a restricted language score higher on non-verbal tests than on verbal. In this case their lack of higher vocabulary stunts their verbal performance but their performance on the non-verbal tests illustrates that they are of equal intelligence with children who score equally well on verbal and non-verbal tests. **(4)**

Bernstein's (1976) research into the cognitive abilities of babies shows that babies can distinguish between focal colours without knowing their names. The babies register a different reaction to each colour, suggesting that some thought process is being undertaken. The above research strongly contradicts the Whorf-Sapir strong linguistic relativity theory. If language determined thought then deaf-mute adults would have no IQ at all and babies would not be capable of any selective skills until they had learned the names of every object involved. Whorf-Sapir cite the Dani Indians who distinguish only between black and white, and the Zuni tribe who do not differentiate between orange and yellow, as evidence for different world views coming about through different language. But, it is not that these tribes cannot see the differences in colours, they do not need to. Rosch (1973) and Brown and Lenneberg taught these tribes to make the differentiation which illustrates that they did not have isolated unchangeable world views. **(5)** So the relationship between thought and language is not a fixed, one-way process, whereby a person's language means that they will think in a specific way. **(6)**

However, there is evidence to support language influencing thought, the weak form or linguistic relativity theory. In an experiment by Carmichael, Hogan, Walters (1932) where verbal labels were given with ambiguous stimuli, the subjects tended to draw not what they had seen but what the verbal label had suggested. This suggests that our language

(3) A brief mention of experimental evidence would back up this point, e.g., the studies made by Bower.

(4) This paragraph runs the risk of ranging over too wide a field, covering as it does neonates, young children, telegraphic speech, deaf-mutes, and class-related language codes. On the other hand it does highlight the variety of evidence that relates to this debate.

(5) The writer quite skilfully summarises the main points about a series of studies of tribes and colour perception. Her understanding of the arguments is demonstrated, without the specific details being presented at length.

(6) The final sentence of this paragraph makes a link back to the specific question.

influences how we store our concepts and how much attention is paid to unfamiliar items. In the Bartlett (1932) serial reproduction experiment western subjects dropped the mystical, spiritual concepts from the story or changed them into 'westernised' concepts which they could understand and relate to better. **(7)**

From the evidence then it can be assumed that thought exists long before language is available and it is possible to think without having access to language. However, once language becomes a part of everyday functioning it can help to facilitate the thinking process. It can give definable terms to our thoughts and make them readily available. Language does, thus, influence thought because we tend to translate our ideas and thoughts into verbal descriptions, but thought will always be the primary function; after all, you can communicate without language but you cannot speak without thought. **(8)**

Jennifer Gunn

(7) These two studies are neatly juxtaposed – one showing the effect of language on concepts and the other, how concepts (relating to culture) influence language (i.e., memory for stories).

(8) The final paragraph makes a real attempt to conclude, coming down on the side of the primacy of thought in the relationship of thought and language.

This essay is particularly *well structured*, with a clear introduction, emphasising the main points of the debate, and a conclusion that follows on well from the evidence presented in the answer. The *content* is wide-ranging – almost too much so in places. Without one or two clear signposts, linking the material back to the question, there would be the danger of the answer becoming confusing. However, the *style* is tight enough, and the expression of ideas sufficiently clear, to ensure that the answer remains relevant.

Discuss the factors involved in interpersonal attraction.

There is an old cliché which says that it is love which makes the world go around. However others beg to differ, such as Rubin McNeil (1983) who believes that liking rather than loving is the more important. There are, however, certain determinants which make people like or love each other; some are characteristic to both, other are exclusive to one. These determinants are: physical attractiveness, similarity in attitudes, personality, reciprocity and proximity. **(1)**

However, there is one overall main theoretical approach to attraction which is called the social exchange theory, introduced by Thibaut and Kelly in the late 1950s. They used a theory adapted from capitalist economics to explain friendship and love. They believed the following idea – we weigh up the costs and benefits of interacting with other people. The costs include such factors as embarrassment, anxiety and irritation. At the same time, dualistically, people are doing exactly the

(1) This paragraph provides quite a lively introduction ending with a list of issues to discuss.

same to us. Thus, we barter our qualities and behaviour when choosing which people we wish to interact with, and are always trying to obtain the best 'deal' for ourselves. We weigh up our own past experiences and knowledge and observations of others we regard as similar to ourselves, what we can hope and expect to receive. Therefore if we find out that what – or rather who – we have is not up to our expectations, and we feel we are not getting what we deserve, then we will find ourselves dissatisfied with the situation and start making attempts to look elsewhere. This theory is intended to apply at all levels, from looking for whom to talk to at a party through to the extremes of looking for a husband or wife. **(2)**

There is very little support for this theory, however, although Price and Vandenberg (1976) did find that the physical attractiveness of married couples in the USA correlated 0.30. **(3)** This shows a slight tendency for people to marry others who are similar to them in physical attractiveness although this is an extremely ambiguous and opinionated result.

The other disadvantage to the theory is that although it is an attempt to explain behaviour it can in no way predict future behaviour. Thus the basic deduction of the theory is that people with 'similar' values will end up together. Thus people would have to be able to put a value on all the qualities about a person. This is surely a matter of opinion and not an entity which can be measured in a regular way.

To investigate friendships Mareno (1931) used sociometry – a method of studying group structures based on certain things and by collecting choices of the most or least preferred members of a group by each individual member. He found that the most popular people were those found to be the healthiest, wealthiest, most intelligent, attractive, sociable and helpful. Obviously there is a great flaw in the experiment and that is that it asks for ideal choices and does not take into account actual, real behaviour. Research into friendships has rested on the following factors: attitude, personality proximity and attractiveness. **(4)**

First, attitudes. Bryne (1971) found that people were more likely to form friendships if they had similar attitudes. Arason and Worchel constructed questionnaires asking for responses from strangers who were either similar or dissimilar to the subjects in their attitudes. The subjects, however, were led to believe that the dissimilar strangers liked them, while the similar strangers disliked them. The subjects rated higher towards the dissimilar strangers who liked them and less to the similar strangers who they believed disliked them. Thus there is evidence here for reciprocal liking.

(2) This is a good synopsis of social exchange theory, even if the phrasing gets a little bit obscure towards the end.

(3) Relevant use of statistics; i.e., it is appropriate for the argument to be backed up occasionally by figures from research.

(4) A good link to the rest of the essay.

Newcombe investigated attitudes with previously unacquainted students who were housed together in groups of 17 for a period of a few months; during this time friendship patterns and attitudes were monitored. In the first experiment Newcombe found the friendships formed initially between room-mates, but later between people with similar attitudes to each other. He also saw people slightly change their own attitudes to match others in a better way. In his second experiment students were specifically selected to share a room with someone who was either similar or dissimilar to them. Unexpectedly the result was that all the room-mates stayed friends. This shows two things; first, that attitudes are important, but also second, that proximity is also important.

The second factor is personality. **(5)** Izard (1960) carried out an experiment whereby unacquainted female students were left to get to know each other. It was found that the three most liked and three least liked all had similar attitudes.

(5) Putting in markers like this keeps the factors being discussed clear.

The third factor is physical attractiveness. Adifoli (1975) found that the least liked group of students in a study when subjects were asked to choose a room-mate from their dorm-mates were on average the most physically attractive. The most wanted and best liked group were those subjects who had previously scored highly on a personality test, but who were less attractive.

To conclude, it shows that no one factor causes friendship, but a mixture of many.

With regard to love, Rubin (1975) studied romantic attraction, and looked at the difference between liking and loving. Using a questionnaire he attempted to discover what the differences were. He concluded that in order to love someone there are certain characteristics which are exclusiveness, absorption, an obsessive want to help and dependency. In other words, if you are in love with someone you will feel attracted to them by a powerful bond, you will be jealous of their relationships with others and would do almost anything for them.

Rubin tested his questionnaire by getting students to fill it in with their current dating partner in mind, and then a friend of the same sex. The questions on the love scale were like 'if I could never be with _____ I'd be miserable' and on the like scale they were like 'when I am with _____ we are always in the same moods'. **(6)**

(6) This is helpful detail.

Walster *et al.* carried out an experiment in the 1960s where previously unacquainted students were given a dating partner for a dance. It was concluded that those partners who found each other physically attractive arranged another date, whilst those who did not made no other arrangements. However at a dance there is no chance for a person's personality to come through anyway. **(7)**

Some psychologists believe that couples ought to have similar attitudes and needs, but Winch (1958) believed that couples ought to have complementary needs. For example, for one half to be dominant, the other to be submissive for a harmonious relationship to exist.

Apart from the above mentioned factors there are two other suggestions as to why people are attracted to each other. **(8)**

First there is non-verbal communication suggested by Argyle (1975). He believed that attributes such as positive tone of voice and eye contact can make a person more attractive. It is highly believed that when a person is sexually aroused his or her pupils will dilate and this in turn has a favourable effect on the other person.

Second, some people believed that pheromones are sexually attractive. These are the chemical odours given off by a person naturally from their day-to-day living. An experiment was carried out in a dentist's waiting room and it was concluded that women sat nearer to a chair which had pheromones sprayed on to it.

Thus, there are evidently many factors which cause inter-personal attractions and it is also evident that it is not merely one of these factors which is outstandingly significant, but a mixture of all of them.

Georgina Meikle

(7) Whether this is more to do with love, or should have been covered earlier in the essay when other studies of attractiveness were considered, is debatable.

(8) While this forms a good link, it suggests that these are extra points that have just occurred to the writer. Perhaps no plan was made?

While the essay is well supplied with sentences that guide the reader through, and link back to the question, the *structure* is a bit loose. Nevertheless, a wide range of studies is covered in a coherent way. The *content* is broad, and there is considerable detail in places. It is all relevant to the question. What is misssing is an analysis at a more conceptual/theoretical level, to put the studies into a broader context. Generally, the *style* is clear with a good blend of illustration and explanation.

The structured question and statistics

In addition to standard essay questions, students are also confronted with questions on statistics and methodology. These are generally in a structured format, requiring a series of brief answers. The approach to questions like this is not the same as answering an essay question. Nor is it like filling in a questionnaire! The clue to tackling questions like this is to look at how they are formulated and what marks are being offered for the question. If there is only one mark going, then the answer almost certainly requires just one clear piece of information. For example:

Question
Define the term population as used in statistics. (*1 mark*)

Answer
Population refers to a group of people or observations which includes all the possible members of that category.

A more elaborate question might carry three or more marks. This will require a fuller answer. The examiner will probably be looking for at least three distinct pieces of information, if three marks are on offer. It is helpful to include brief examples to back up any points that you are making to indicate that you have understood the question.
For example:

Question
What is a repeated measures design and what are its advantages? (*3 marks*)

Answer
A repeated measures design is one way of approaching an experiment. In a repeated measures or within-groups design, the subjects undertake both the conditions of the experiment. For example, in an experiment on the Muller-Lyer illusion they may judge the length of the line in both the horizontal and the vertical condition. The main advantage of this design is that each subject acts as their own control. They are perfectly matched with themselves. Another advantage is that only half the number of subjects is needed compared to an independent measures design.

In this answer the term has been defined and a brief example given. Two advantages have been highlighted. The question does not ask for disadvantages, so these need not be given.

With structured questions, there is generally a stimulus passage describing an experiment. This should be read carefully, *at least twice* before you start answering the questions. Often the answers to at least some of the questions are contained directly in the passage. If they

are not there directly, then there may well be a clue as to how to pro-
ceed.

There are two further parts of this book designed to help with questions of this type. The section of questions starting on page 137 is
designed to tackle most parts of an introductory syllabus on experimental methods. It is recommended that they should be answered
prior to looking at the guidance on answers given at the end of the
book. The final section of the book gives indications as to what could
be included in answers rather than specific 'model answers'. The section on statistics (pages 58–114) is *not* intended to be a comprehensive text on statistics, but rather an introduction and an overview. It
should be used in conjunction with one of the many excellent introductory texts on statistics that are available.

Types of practical

The most usual type of practical undertaken is the experiment. However, there are three other types of practical which we can consider; namely, the observation, the correlation and the case study. We will consider each in turn.

The experiment

The experiment follows the traditional scientific model. In a study of this sort a specific hypothesis is being tested about the causal effect of a particular variable. For example, it might be predicted that a noisy environment would have an impact on the performance of a mathematical test. The alternate or experimental hypothesis might be 'that the scores on a mathematical test will be significantly higher when it is taken in a quiet environment, than when taken in a noisy environment'. The independent variable (IV) would be the type of environment, and the dependent variable (DV) would be the scores achieved on the maths test. This is therefore a test of differences – that is the effect that *different* values or conditions of the IV will have on the DV. Strictly, in an experiment, it is the null hypothesis that is being tested. This would state that 'there will be no significant difference between the scores obtained for the maths test in the noisy environment or in the quiet environment'. The null hypothesis is falsifiable. If it is proved wrong in the experiment, then it is possible to *support* the experimental hypothesis (note: we do not say *prove*).

In an experiment the investigator is seeking to establish the *causal link* between the two variables being investigated. Hence this type of design is known as a causal design. A causal design requires that the independent variable can be manipulated. This condition does not really apply to a correlation.

Correlation and other non-causal designs

A correlation or test of association looks at the relationship between variables. Here the interest is in how the change in one variable is associated with the change in another variable. If we wished to establish whether there was a possible link between lead pollution and intelligence, we might measure the distance children live from a major road and see if it correlated with their intelligence as measured by an IQ test. We might be interested to test out Rokeach's idea of dogmatism and prejudice. Here we would look at people's score on a dogmatism scale and see how it related to their score on a measure of racism and sexism. We would need, in each case, to control for other possible variables that might influence the outcome. In the first, the income of the parents and how long the child had lived in their house would be among the most relevant. In the second, educational level or intelligence might be important variables to control for. In both cases – and indeed with all correlations – we cannot assume that an association means a causal link.

It is because correlations are not causal designs that we cannot really talk about an IV and a DV in this context. The two variables may not be related at all. For example, there is probably a positive correlation between the age of marriage and the sale of pop records. Both may well have risen over the last ten years. However, we cannot assume any necessary relationship (although there may be a loose link) in terms of changes in the economy.

When designing a correlational study (and writing about it) it is important to specify what the variables are that are being studied. Also, it may be that you will assume the possibility that one is more fundamental (causal) than the other. This can be treated as approximating an IV. However, you need to bear in mind that neither a positive nor a negative correlation demonstrates a causal link.

There are other experimental designs which are also, strictly, non-causal. They do not really constitute correlations either as they are tests of difference. These non-causal designs occur when the IV cannot really be manipulated. An example of this is a comparison of males and females for a given psychological characteristic. For example, if we compared the skill of males and females on a manual dexterity test, we do not manipulate the sex as a variable, we just use an independent measures design. We cannot say that sex differences *cause* differences in manual dexterity. It may well be some other factor altogether, like socialisation. Because no direct cause can be assumed, this type of design is also non-causal. However, in all other respects it can be treated as an experiment.

Non-experimental methods and observational studies

Non-experimental methods would include observations, surveys and case studies. Students may well wish to experience one or more of these firsthand, as the approaches differ in a number of respects from an experiment.

Survey

This is used where direct observation is not possible. Kinsey's famous survey of sexual behaviour and the Newson and Newson study of child-rearing approaches are two prominent examples of this technique. The careful selection of a suitable sample, and the administration of interviews or questionnaires, are the main techniques involved here. Attitude surveys, adapted or developed by students, can provide interesting and challenging practical work.

The case study

Freud made particular use of this approach. His in-depth description of the psychological functioning of 'The Wolf Man' is a particularly striking example. This analysis, completed in 1915, delved into the biography and childhood experiences and relationships of one man. It sought to explain his adult manic-depression, in terms of various childhood neuroses. In the case study, then, the focus shifts to the individual. It is an *idiographic* approach: in other words it is a qualitative description of individual factors influencing behaviour. It tends to concentrate on what is unique in the experience of one person.

Another example is provided by the highly readable study of *Sybil* by Schreiber (1973). This describes the possible causes of multiple personality in a young woman. Again the current behaviour and therapeutic treatment is explored in terms of childhood trauma.

A case study is not an easy form of study to accomplish successfully by students. If it is undertaken, considerable thought should be given to what the form of the study will be, and how evidence will be recorded. Without a clear direction a case study can just end up as a diffuse description.

The observation

This is an important psychological technique, which differs substantially from the laboratory-based experiment. The work of ethologists like Lorenz and Tinbergen have demonstrated the value of this approach in relation to studies of animals. Festinger (1956), who joined a sect that believed the world was imminently due to end, showed how useful such in depth study would be. His theory of cognitive dissonance developed, in part, out of that study to explain the response of the cult members when the world did not end.

Festinger's work can be described as *participant observation*, because he participated covertly as a sect member. Many observation studies may be covert, in so far as those observed are not aware they are being studied, but students are less likely to be involved in full-blown participant observation studies. It will be helpful to look in some detail at the methods and techniques involved in observational studies.

Observation – some basic techniques

Observations require careful planning. Anyone in doubt on this point should choose any social situation and try 'just observing' for a few minutes. The vast variety of things occurring means that what is observed has to be a selection. Any two people just observing the same scene will actually 'see' different things.

The observation needs to be structured and organised in terms of a specific problem or hypothesis. Indeed some observations can be considered as 'natural experiments'. These we will consider first.

Field experiment

A field experiment is one that is carried out in 'the field'; in other words, it is not laboratory based. The experimenter uses a natural setting. The participants may not know they are part of an experiment. The experimenter will manipulate some variable to see what the effect is. An example is the Hofling study of obedience, when he observed nurses on a hospital ward.

Natural experiment

This is similar to a field experiment, except the observer does not intervene directly with a manipulation of any variables. The variables occur naturally. The observation of non-verbal behaviour in crowded or only partially full train carriages would be an example. The independent variable would be the number of people present.

Organising and recording data

As observations are so open-ended, a way of organising data is imperative. The data need to be recorded in a systematic fashion. For example, if you were going to investigate the fixed action patterns of a rat, you might record the rat's behaviour every five seconds, on some sort of checklist. In this way you would have a record both of the frequency of types of behaviour and their sequence.

Certain techniques that help with organising data are:

event sampling
time sampling
rating scales

1 Event sampling
This is where every time a particular behaviour occurs it is recorded. In order to do this a list of possible behaviours needs to be drawn up first. Then a check or tick can be made on each occasion a specific behaviour is undertaken.

2 Time sampling
Again this requires a checklist. As in the fixed action patterns example given above, the predominant behaviour in any given time period is recorded. This can be used for observing single subjects or groups.

3 Rating scales
For given types of behaviour a series of scales is developed. Then the observer will complete these scales for individuals or groups. For example, if observing a group of children, scales might be produced for aggressive behaviour, co-operative activity, degree to which they ask for help, initiate activity, talk and so on. The scale could be five or seven check points, with guidance like 'always talking, talks sometimes, seldom talks'. At the end there will be a profile for each participant for each of these characterisics.

Other techniques could involve the following:

1 Using a video camera
This can be particularly effective for recording group interactions. It means that behaviour can be analysed carefully after the event. However, the video itself is too 'raw' as it stands and the data in it may need to be organised, using one of the methods already discussed.

2 Using a camera
This can catch key moments in a behavioural sequence. It is a technique that can be used to back up other forms of observation.

3 Using a tape recorder
This could be used to monitor behaviour, e.g., the questions a teacher directs to boys as compared to girls in a class. An accurate record like this allows precise analysis of language used. Also small, portable tape recorders could be used to allow verbal descriptions of behaviour as the observation takes place. They will be a bit like a sports commentary. The problem with this method is that the material will have to be transcribed later, which is a time-consuming process.

4 Making sketches
Swift diagrams or sketches are another method by which observations can be captured. These could be done, for example, for a time sample of where children are in a room relating to various toys or stimuli.

When data have been collected, they need to be effectively presented. Often descriptive statistics can be used – for example, histograms or pie charts. If the observation has involved cameras, tape recorders, or written or sketched accounts, then quotations, extracts or summaries of these can be effectively used. The important consideration here is that a careful distinction must be made between what has been actually observed and the interpretations of the observer. As Stern (1930) argued, in considering observations of children, no conclusions should be drawn which cannot be positively justified by the actual observation.

Experiments in psychology

The following pages give brief outlines of a number of possible practicals. They have been deliberately left a little open-ended, so that the construction of suitable hypotheses and the development of a full procedure will need to be worked out by the student. Each of the suggestions has been tried successfully by students.

The first examples are of observation studies on children. These are covered in some detail, and should be read in conjunction with the section on observation (see pages 47–49).

Studying children: use of observation

It is a very enjoyable function for students of a course in Psychology to spend some time doing a study on an aspect of developmental psychology. This is often an excellent opportunity to undertake an observation. A letter or a personal approach to a play group or primary school will usually result in permission being granted, if you have a clear idea of what it is you want to study, and how you will go about it.

It is possible to undertake an experimental design, and to test out, for example, some of Piaget's experiments, and those of his critics (see pages 23–28). The design will usually be independent measures, comparing different age groups. However, we will consider an observational study. You need to decide which aspect of the children's behaviour you wish to observe. Two examples will be considered here. The first will investigate types of play. The second will focus on interaction patterns in groups.

1 Children's play

You will need to take a theory about children's play, and decide which aspect you wish to investigate. This will be influenced by the children you have access to, their ages, and the situation in which you will be observing them. A preliminary visit to your school or group is therefore very important.

You might wish to focus on the difference between ordinary play and challenging play (see Sylva and Lundt, *Child Development: a First Course*, 1982, pp. 164–170). In challenging play the activities are more demanding, whereas ordinary play is simpler, requiring fewer skills and less use of the imagination.

Apparatus

The important factor in a naturalistic observation is the observation schedule. This is a record of the activities that you observe. It allows behaviour to be classified and recorded against time. In the diagram the type of schedule used by Sylva *et al.* in their observation study is given. Such a schedule allows quick notes to be made, while observing, and for a pattern of behaviour to be built up over time. Each column needs only to have brief notes, minute by minute. For example under 'Social setting' might go 'solitary', 'child pair' 'small group', 'large group'. With 'play' a few categories would be developed from your initial observations (e.g., 'pretend play', 'small scale construction' etc.). With 'language', codes could be used to indicate the target child (TC) another child (OC) or an adult (A).

Minute	Activity	Language used	Social setting	Play theme

(Adapted from Sylva and Lundt)

Procedure

You still need to give thought to your design, in the sense that you may wish to compare different naturalistic settings. The variables you might deal with could include age, free play *vs* organised play, sex of children playing, types of toys available, time of day and so on.

The schedule you use should be tested out and adapted if necessary. You could back it up with use of other recording devices; e.g., a tape recorder, camera or video. It is best if the children can get used to your presence a bit before you start your observation or you may become the key variable determining their behaviour.

Results and statistics

The results for an observation differ from those of an experiment, for you are unlikely to use inferential statistics. You may use some descriptive statistics, but generally your findings will be composed of verbal descriptions. These should be organised to illustrate the particular aspect of the children's activity you were investigating. If it is a contrast between simple and complex play, then various short descriptive passages could provide 'pen sketches' of the points you wish to illustrate.

By all means include diagrams, photos, brief transcriptions from tape or video, but make sure that what you include is demonstrably relevant to the theme of your study.

2 *Leadership in children's groups*

A more formal study using older children could use Bales' schedule of leadership behaviour in groups, or any other suitable classificatory scheme. Bales' scheme is based on analysing people's behaviour in terms of the emotional area and the task area. The emotional area is analysed in terms of positive and negative reactions. The task area is scored in terms of asking questions and attempting answers. Such a study would benefit from the use of a video camera, to allow for a more detailed analysis of interactions but this is not vital, especially if the observation is being carried out by a team. The group or groups of children will need to be given a suitable discussion topic or problem to solve.

Apparatus

Again, an observation schedule needs to be devised which focuses on the issues of interest eg leadership behaviour. A video camera which can record the whole group, with chairs suitably arranged (e.g., in a crescent shape), will be valuable. Alternatively, a tape recorder could be used, but it may prove difficult to be sure who is speaking.

Procedure

Time needs to be given to allow the group to settle down before starting the observation. The children will need to be very clear about the problem they are to discuss, how long they have to come to a decision, and any other 'ground rules' they need to be told about. Make sure you check that your video/tape recorder is actually recording. Nothing is more frustrating than completing your observations only to find the microphone was not switched on!

Results and statistics

As with the previous observation study, these will need to be tailored to the specific issue you are investigating. If you have compared groups, you may wish to present your results showing:

a) the similarities between each group,
b) the differences that occur.

Use of suitable quotes, diagrams and descriptions should illustrate the points you wish to make, relating to the basic hypotheses you are investigating.

Sight, sound and dexterity

A very simple design can be used to test the proposition that the presence of sound influences motivation and skill in playing video games. This experiment would touch on perception, physiological psychology, motivation and possibly learning theory.

Apparatus

You will need access to a computer and a suitable computer game or two – where sound is used. With a suitable room, a stop clock and pencil and paper to record results, you will be under way.

Procedure

You need to take care over your design. You will have to *counterbalance* in order to control for *order effect*, if you use a repeated measures design. This is preferable as the variation in experience and skill with computer games is considerable. A matched subjects design or independent measures design could be used, but would probably need to involve considerably more subjects.

A trial run will be valuable to ensure that your instructions are clear and that the games are neither so easy that you get a '*floor effect*', nor so difficult that you have a '*ceiling effect*' in your measurements.

One other problem will be subjects guessing what the experiment is about and so producing a self-fulfilling prophecy (or an experiment with '*demand characteristics*' (see page 180). You will need an explanation with modest subterfuge!

Results

The results will be scores that will probably achieve interval status. You will need to check if your overall data are parametric. Then, depending on your design, you will need a suitable test of difference.

Selective attention and personal stereos

The availability of stereo tape recorders, and the portability of personal stereos, means that it is possible to replicate a number of the classic studies of selective attention, testing the theories of Broadbent, Treisman, Deutsch and Deutsch, and Norman. Although the theories differ, the apparatus remains much the same.

Apparatus

You will need either to obtain a stereo recording system on which you can record separate messages on the two different stereo channels, or to use two portable stereos. In the second case one stereo carries one message and the other the second. You will have to use some ingenuity with the headphones to ensure the correct message goes to the appropriate ear. This experiment stands or falls on the choice of material that you record and the quality of the recording, so care should be taken over this.

Procedure

This is another instance where a careful pilot study is essential, first to make sure that you are confident with the apparatus, and second to test that it works in the way that you expect it will. Your design will probably be independent measures, as you are likely to want to use the same stimulus materials, but require the groups of subjects to do different things with it. As subjects can be a bit embarrassed doing 'shadowing task' (where they say aloud what they hear in one ear), you may need to take time putting them at their ease, and choosing a suitable place to carry out the experiment.

Results

The data you obtain may be of interval status; you will need to decide if they really are more than just ordinal. If your design is independent measures then your choice will be between an independent t-test (if the data are parametric) or a Mann-Whitney.

Your results would include examples of the sort of errors made in the shadowing tasks, if these appear to be relevant to the hypothesis that you are testing.

First impressions

Asch, in a classic experiment in 1946, investigated the effects of first impressions. He gave his participants one of two descriptions that related to a hypothetical person. The first list read:

intelligent, industrious, impulsive, critical, stubborn, envious;

the second reversed the order:

envious, stubborn, critical, impulsive, industrious, intelligent.

Asch found that participants given the first list responded more favourably to the person than those who received the second list. They appeared to be influenced by a *primacy* effect. The words read first, Asch argued, influenced how later words were interpreted.

Apparatus

It is quite possible to replicate Asch's experiment, using the same, or similar words. One of my students was interested to try a visual version, where a character is seen as behaving in two contrasting ways. The pictures he used are reproduced on pages 56 and 57. In each the essential story is the same; it is just the order which is changed.

Procedure

Having shown participants the version that is positive first or the version that is negative first, they will be invited to make an assessment of the personality of the main character, Metro. This can be done in an *open-ended* way, where they will be asked to write about the character. External judges will then have to assess the descriptions to decide how far they are positive or negative about the character. This can be done on a scale (which could range from 1 – *positive* to 7 – *negative*). Needless to say, the judges should not know which sequence of pictures the participants have seen. Another method that is effective is to invite participants to choose (say) five words from a list of (say) forty. The words could be made up of fifteen negative words, fifteen that are positive and ten that are neutral. The word list should be drawn up with the help of judges who were not directly involved in the experiment. Each word would carry a score (either +1 positive or −1 negative or 0 neutral). More elaborate forms of scoring may suggest themselves to you. The hypothesis would be that participants who see the positive version first will rate the lead character more favourably than those who see the negative version first.

Results and statistics

The data generated will be ordinal. As the scores are not necessarily paired and as the design has to be independent measures, a Mann-Whitney U test is an appropriate form of statistics to use.

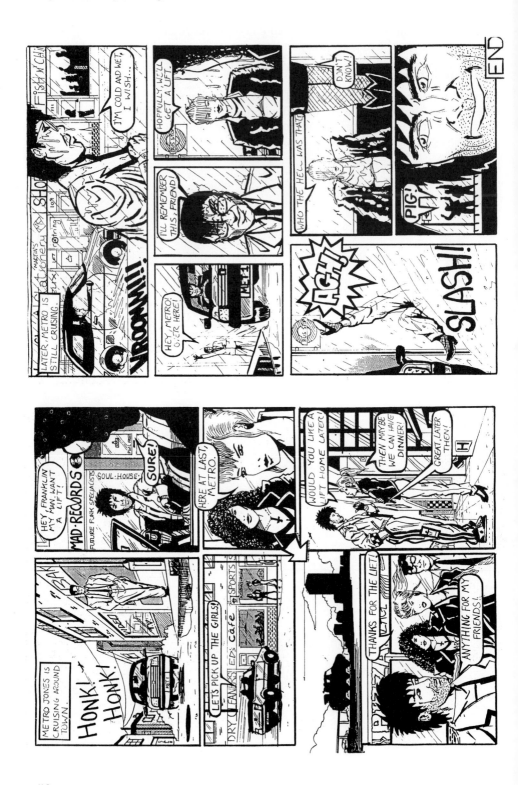

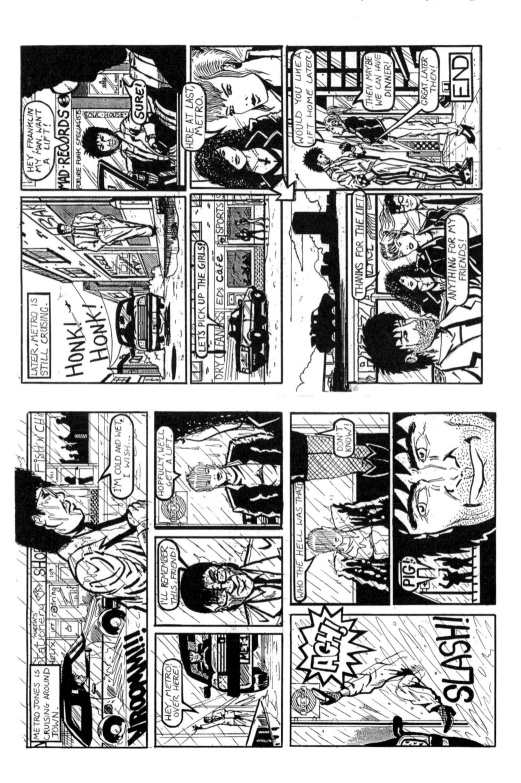

57

Simple guide to statistics

In order successfully to plan your practical work and effectively design an experiment, you need to be aware of the statistical procedures you will be using. This next section is designed to aid you in this process. It provides a 'survivors's guide' to statistics, and is designed to provide basic information and procedures for most of the statistics you are likely to need on an introductory course. However, there is not space in a small volume such as this to go fully into the background of the statistical terms and tests. There are a number of good books currently easily available to students. For those of you who wish to understand the *why* of the statistical procedures set out later in this chapter, I would recommend that you follow up in one of these other texts.

Aspects of statistics covered in this section are
- levels of measurement
- description and organisation of data
- the normal distribution
- probability
- sampling
- problems, guessing and proof
- choosing and using statistical tests
- how to use statistical tables

Levels of measurement

When an observation or experiment is completed there will be data. If the data are numerical they can be considered to have different levels of precision. If we categorise people as smokers or non-smokers or if we consider French, German and English people, we cannot put a numerical value on these categories. They are just names. Such data are nominal. The order of finalists in a beauty contest or the rating we give to different types of beer will give us mathematical data. These we can put in rank order, but we cannot say precisely how much more one is preferred than another. We just know their relative position. These data are ordinal. Where we have scores from a test, for example an IQ test or a test of neuroticism, the data are in units. We can assume each unit on the scale is of equal size. These are interval data.

Nominal – data in categories and a measure of frequency.
Ordinal – data that can be put in rank order.
Interval – data measured on a scale of equal units.

Nominal data When data are not numerical as such, and cannot be put into rank order, then they are *nominal*. In other words things are just named or put into categories. Examples would include smokers and non-smokers; males and females; vegetarians, fish eaters and meat eaters. In the picture above, the categories might be 'neat' and 'scruffy'.

Ordinal data When it is possible to put data into ranks, then they are *ordinal*. This is when it is possible to talk about degrees of something. A beauty contest sorts the contestants into order of beauty, as decided by the judges, but although they may be 'first', 'second' and 'third', this does not mean that you can say exactly *how much* more beautiful one is than another. Similarly, we can arrange people according to their height. If we just talk of short, medium and tall, then these are ordinal data. If, however, we actually measure them, in centimetres or inches, then the data are of a more precise nature and are called *interval*.

There is a fourth type of data, ratio, which is where the scale is interval, but where there is an absolute zero. Time is an example, as is length and weight. It is very doubtful that any psychological test produces ratio data.

Interval data Where data are made up of numbers that come from a scale of equal intervals, then these are *interval* data. In the cartoon, the intervals are hamburgers and a less bizarre example would be inches, or seconds, or grams. It is debatable whether any purely psychological measures can be considered to produce truly interval data. However, scores on personality inventories and IQ tests are treated as interval data, and many psychology experiments do result in measures of time, which are interval. Deciding whether data have reached interval status, if they are in terms of scores from some psychological test, is not always easy. In writing a practical report, your choice in this regard will often need to be justified.

> Independent variable (IV) – This is the variable that is expected to produce a change in another variable. By manipulating this variable the experimenter sees if a change is produced in the dependent variable.

For example, in an experiment on memory, the independent variable may be whether the group has been advised to make mental images of words given in a list or not. The dependent variable is then the number of words remembered under the two conditions. Statistics can be used to see if it is possible to infer whether any differences in the two scores can be explained by the effect of the IV rather than chance.

> Dependent variable (DV) – This is the variable that is affected, or may be affected, by the IV.

Parametric and non-parametric tests

Parametric tests can use the properties of the normal curve of distribution and the related characteristics of the standard deviation. For a test to be parametric it must meet three criteria, relating to (a) the level of measurement, (b) the variance and (c) the type of distribution. Remember that tests are inferring either differences between data or relationships (correlation) between data. To use parametric tests, the data must, in effect, relate to 'populations'. If they do not, or if the two sets of data have very different parameters (i.e., come from very dissimilar populations), then non-parametric tests must be used.

> Parametric tests require
> (1) Data   – that are at least of interval status
> (2) Distribution – two sets of scores that conform closely to the normal curve of distribution
> (3) Variability – both sets of scores having a similar variance (or standard deviation).

Parametric tests	*Non-parametric tests*
Related t-test	Wilcoxon (also Sign test)
Independent t-test	Mann-Whitney
Pearson's Product Moment	Spearman's rho
	Chi^2

Robustness and sensitivity

Finally, before considering in detail how to choose a test, their relative merits should be considered. Obviously, the more the smaller variables in data can be monitored or registered by a test, the more sensitive a test will be. On these grounds the Chi^2 test and the Sign test are quite crude. However, it is very difficult to get 'ideal' data that completely meet the requirements of mathematical theory. So, tests that can handle data which are a bit 'rough and ready' are known as robust.

Statisticians debate at great length the relative merits of parametric and non-parametric tests. Generally though, the principle holds that the non-parametric tests are more robust, whilst the parametric tests are more sensitive. The sensitivity of parametric tests means that they are also more powerful.

Description and organisation of data

In an experiment to investigate the role of insight in solving a maze, a student obtained the following data. The experimental group were shown a maze for one minute and invited to study it. The control group were not given any preview of the maze. The experimental hypothesis was that looking at the maze for one minute, before attempting to solve it, would produce a quicker solution than not having such a preview. The results were as follows:

Participants in 'insight' group	Time in secs	Participants in control group	Time in secs
P1	60	P16	75
P2	62	P17	108
P3	57	P18	109
P4	42	P19	95
P5	95	P20	85
P6	57	P21	110
P7	91	P22	84
P8	35	P23	53
P9	77	P24	40
P10	130	P25	123
P11	43	P26	180
P12	146	P27	47
P13	139	P28	93
P14	163	P29	101
P15	39	P30	58

A brief study of these initial data does not reveal whether seeing the maze beforehand led to a swifter solution overall. The data need to be organised in an effective way to allow comparison. We will first look at mathematical ways of summarising the data. We will then consider some graphical ways in which the data may be represented.

Measures of central tendency of scores

We will consider three measures of central tendency. Each gives us some information about the 'middleness' of scores.

Mean

The first is what is commonly referred to as the average. This is a valuable summary of all the data in a set of scores as it takes account of each value.

> The mean of a set of numbers or scores is the sum of all the scores divided by the number of scores in the set.

Median

As its name suggests, this is the number that has the same number of scores above it as below it, when the scores have been put in rank order. This is particularly useful where there are a few extreme scores. The median is not distorted by such scores.

> The median is the value of the central score in a distribution of scores arranged in rank order.

Mode

The score or scores that occur most often in a set are modal. The mode is of most value in dealing with frequency data, where nominal levels of measurement are being used. Here the most frequent category is useful information.

> The mode is the most frequently occurring score in a given distribution of scores.

Mean

Calculations

Example

The calculation using the data given for the 'insight group' above.

Step 1

Add all the scores in the series together to get the total.

Step 1

$\Sigma x = 1236$

Step 2

Divide by the total number of scores in the series.
The result is the mean.

The formula for this is:

$$\frac{\Sigma x}{N}$$

where
Σ = the total of the scores or 'the sum of'
x = each score
N = the number of scores in the set
$\bar{x}$ = mean

Step 2

$$\frac{\Sigma x}{N} = \frac{1236}{15}$$

$$\bar{x} = 82.4$$

Median

Calculations

Step 1

Arrange all the data in rank order from smallest to largest.

Step 2

Count all the scores.

Step 3

If there is an uneven number of scores then the median is the middle score.

Step 4

If there is an even number of scores, then the median is the average of the two central scores.

Example

Step 1

35, 39, 42, 43, 57, 57, 60, 62, 77, 91, 95, 130, 139, 146, 163

Step 2

$N = 15$

Step 3

middle score = the 8th score out of 15

median score = 62

Step 4

If there was one further score of, say, 170 in the series above, then the two middle scores would be 62 and 77. The median would be:

$$\frac{62 + 77}{2}$$

$$= 69.5$$

Measures of spread of scores

A set of results or scores does not only have a central tendency but also a degree or amount by which they are dispersed. This is the amount of scattering of the scores.

Range

One way of considering the dispersion or variability of the scores is the range. This is the simplest measure of 'spreadoutness'.

> The range is the difference between the largest and the smallest scores in a distribution.

The range is a rough-and-ready measure, because it takes account only of the two end scores and ignores all the data in the middle. A more sensitive measure is called the variance.

Variance and standard deviation

The variance is closely related to a statistic called the standard deviation. What these two statistics provide is a measure or value, which represents the spread of all the scores around the mean.

> The variance and the standard deviation are measures of the dispersion or variability of a set of scores around the mean. A more formal definition of the variance is the average of the squared deviations of the scores around the mean. The standard deviation is the square root of the variance.

Variance   In the cartoons there are two groups of people waiting at bus stops. If we were to measure their heights and find the average, we might discover that the *mean* height was exactly the same for both. This descriptive statistic is, therefore, not enough adequately to describe these two samples. We need a statistic that will pick out their differences. This is the *variance*. With this measure, the differences in height of the circus group will show up in contrast to the similarity in height of the ballerinas.

Variance and standard deviation

Calculations

Step 1

Arrange the scores in participant order (or rank order).

Step 2

Calculate the mean.

Step 3

Subtract each score from the mean. (Some of the results will be minus figures.)

Step 4

Square the results of step 3. (Multiply each number by itself.)

Step 5

Add together the results of step 4.

Example

Steps 1 to 5

Partici-pants	Scores	Mean – Scores	Square of Mean – Scores
	X	$\bar{X} - X$	$(\bar{X} - X)^2$
P1	60	22.4	501.76
P2	62	20.4	416.16
P3	57	25.4	645.16
P4	42	40.4	1632.16
P5	95	−12.6	158.76
P6	57	25.4	645.16
P7	91	−8.6	73.96
P8	35	47.4	2246.76
P9	77	5.4	29.16
P10	130	−47.6	2265.76
P11	43	39.4	1552.36
P12	146	−63.6	4044.96
P13	139	−56.6	3203.56
P14	163	−80.6	6496.36
P15	39	43.4	1883.56
Total	**1236**	**0**	**25795.6**

Step 6

Divide the result of step 4 by the number of scores.
The result is the variance.

Step 6

$$\frac{25795.6}{15} = 1719.71$$

variance = 1719.71

Step 7

Standard deviation (sd)
The standard deviation is the square root of the variance (use a calculator).

Step 7

standard deviation $= \sqrt{\text{variance}}$

standard deviation $= \sqrt{1719.71}$

$$\text{sd} = 41.47$$

Range

Calculations	Example
Range can be calculated in two ways.	Using the example of the 'insight' group given above: the smallest score is 35 and the largest score is 163.

Method 1

It is the scores described from the lowest to the highest.	The **range** is from 35 to 163.

Method 2

The range can also be computed by finding the difference between the highest and lowest score.	The **range** is $163 - 35$ $= 128$

A frequency tally

This will show the number of times that a given score, or a given range of scores, occurs. This is a necessary stage of analysis before a bar chart can be drawn. The data needs to be organised into appropriate groupings. In the case of the 'insight' group these might be:

Scores in range	Tally	Frequency
31– 60	ⱵꞱ́ II	7
61– 90	II	2
91– 120	II	2
121– 150	III	3
151 +	I	1

A stem and leaf display

The disadvantage of the frequency table above is that a certain amount of data is lost. This is overcome by a useful device called a stem and leaf display. This has the advantage of every figure being part of a graphical representation. The data above are too spread out for this technique to be usefully employed. We will consider scores from an experiment on memory. This experiment tested Craik and Tulving's (1975) theory of levels of processing. The experimenter compared memory for words, where it had been noted if they were in capitals or not (the *shallow* condition), with memory for words whose meaning had been focused on (the *deep* condition). The results were as follows:

Numbers of words remembered by participants

Participants	P1	P2	P3	P4	P5	P6	P7	P8	P9	P10
Conditions										
'Shallow'	5	11	6	10	12	6	9	7	8	12
'Deep'	4	14	8	12	15	10	14	13	12	13

Calculations

Step 1

The stem will often be in units of 10 for two-digit numbers. 0–9 will be on a stem of 0; 10–19 will be on a stem of 1, and so on.

Step 2

The leaves will be the last digit of each number.

Step 3

The stem can be smaller if this is appropriate, in steps of five for example.

Step 4

Numbers can be arranged in rank order within each part of the stem.

Step 5

Two sets of scores can be compared by being placed back to back.

Step 6

(For three-figure numbers, the stem will be the first two digits.)

Example

Using the figures given above, for the experiment on memory:

shallow

0	5 6 6 9 7 8
1	1 0 2 2

deep

0	4 8
1	4 2 5 0 4 3 2 3

Using steps of 5 for the stem, and putting the figures in rank order, we can make this comparison:

'Shallow'		**'Deep'**
	0	4
5 6 6 7 8 9	0	8
0 1 2 2	1	0 2 2 3 3 4 4
	1	5

The differences in the two distributions of scores are now very clear.

A box and whisker comparison

Another way of arranging data makes use of the middle 50% of the scores, as well as the range. It allows data from different groups to be compared graphically. The data are first arranged in rank order. The scores are divided into four equal sets. These are called *quartiles*. A quartile is one quarter of the total number of scores. The two middle quartiles make up the middle 50% of the scores. This is the *box*. The range provides the *whiskers*. The method of calculating quartiles is essentially the same as for working out the median (see above). Box and whisker presentations are generally used to *compare* two or more sets of data.

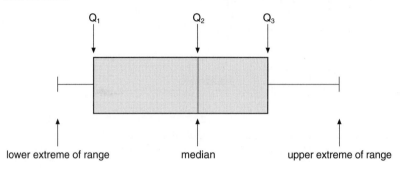

Calculations	Example

Calculations

Example

Using the data for two groups solving the maze:

Step 1

Arrange the data in rank order.

Step 1

'Insight' group
35, 39, 42, 43, 57, 57, 60, 62, 77, 91, 95, 130, 139, 146, 163

Step 2

Divide the total number of scores by two and establish the *median* (Q_2).

Step 2

The median for the 'insight' group is 62.

Step 3

Establish the midpoint of the upper half of the scores (called Q_3).

Step 3

For the 'insight' group the upper quartile (Q_3) is 130. (There are seven scores *above* the median, and 130 is in the middle position.)

Step 4

Repeat for the lower half of the data.

Step 4

Similarly, the lower quartile (Q_1) is 43.

Step 5

Repeat Steps 1 to 4 for each set of data.

Step 5

For the control group Q_1 is 58, Q_2 is 93 and Q_3 is 109.

Step 6

Plot the data as shown.

Step 6

See below.

So for the data for the maze-solving experiment, the box and whisker plot would look like this:

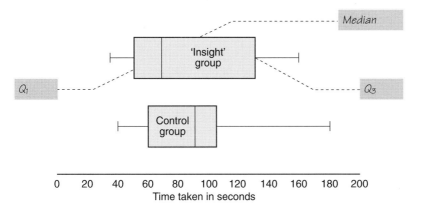

This shows quite clearly that although the range was bigger for the control group, the middle 50% of the scores were more bunched around the median.

Charts

There are various ways in which data may be charted. In each case the frequency of the data will be put on the 'y' axis of the chart, and the numerical value of the data on the 'x' axis.

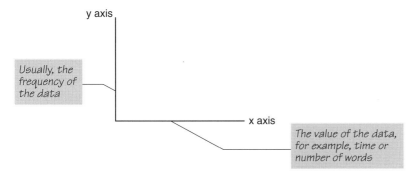

It can be tempting to provide charts where the 'x' axis is the participants. Do not. It is virtually meaningless.

A simple form of chart is a **frequency polygon**. The points on a chart like this can only be joined when the data are in some sense **continuous**, that is, at least of ordinal status (i.e. can be put in rank order, see page 103).

Frequency polygon

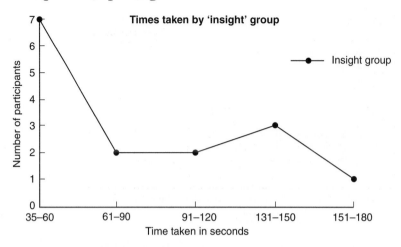

As a **histogram** represents data that are sequential, there should be no gaps between the bars (except where the frequency of a score is zero). The bars should be of equal width.

Histogram

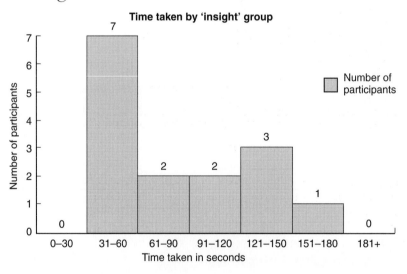

A histogram provides a useful way of comparing data collected under more than one condition. Bar charts for each group can be plotted next to each other and their distributions compared visually.

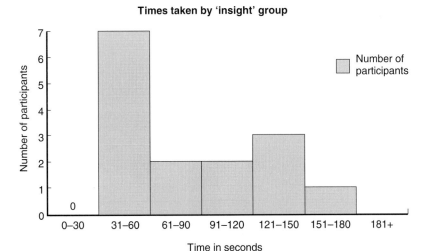

Times taken by 'insight' group

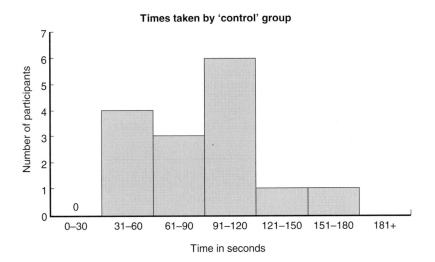

Times taken by 'control' group

Where **nominal** data are being dealt with, then a **bar chart** is appropriate. For example, where students have been observed choosing meals in a canteen, the preferences are at the nominal level. Note that the 'y' axis is still *frequency*. The bars are presented separated from each other.

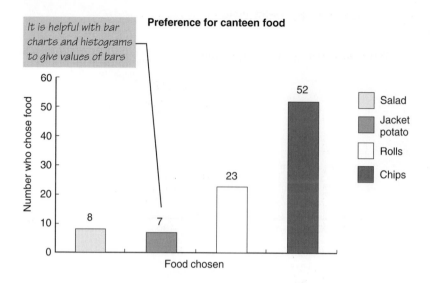

Other methods of presenting data include **pie charts** and **scatter-grams** (see pages 104–107). We will conclude this section on how data may be organised and described with a table, showing the type of tables, charts and simple descriptive statistics that are often appropriate with each type of data.

Type of data	Descriptive statistics	Tables and charts
Nominal	Percentages Mode	Frequency table Pie chart Bar chart
Ordinal	Percentages Median	Frequency table Frequency polygon Scattergram
Interval and ratio	Mean Median Mode Quartiles Range Variance Standard deviation	Frequency table Stem and leaf Box and whisker Histogram Scattergram

The normal curve of distribution

We investigate the height of the adult population in a particular town. We would expect to find that there are a few really tall people, a few very short people, and most people closer to the average height. The distribution of this natural phenomenon – height – can be described as 'normal'. If we collect a lot of data, we could produce a bar chart of people's heights that would begin to show a character-istic pattern.

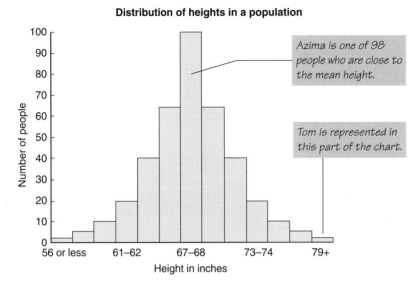

This chart represents the height of nearly 400 people. Tom, who is six feet seven inches tall, is the tallest person in our sample. Azima, who is five feet seven and a half inches tall, is to be found in the middle of the distribution. It is helpful to remember, when dealing with the normal curve, that places on the distribution represent the actual scores of people.

If we were to carry out a survey of intelligence in our community, and we tested about 1,000 adults, then we would find a similar distrib-ution of scores. Most would cluster around the average; we would have a few very bright individuals and a few who scored low on the intelligence test. By convention, the scores for IQ (intelligence quo-tient), range between 0 and 200. An IQ of 100 is considered to be exactly the average.

The distribution of IQ scores in an adult population

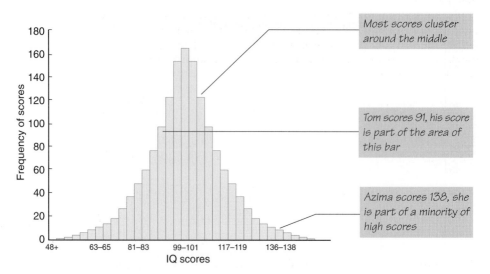

As we can see from the chart above, the distribution of scores for a characteristic like IQ begins to take a distinctive shape. This is known as 'the bell-shaped curve' or the normal curve of distribution. Charts derived empirically, through collecting data, as the one above, will always be somewhat different from the mathematical ideal. However, the more scores that are included, the more the curve will tend towards the mathematical (or Gaussian) curve. (Gauss was a mathematician who studied its properties.)

The normal curve of distribution had distinct properties.
• It is bell shaped and symmetrical around the mean.
• The mean, median and mode all fall on the same central line.
• The curves tend towards the base line but never touch the base line.
These characteristics apply to the mathematical rather than the empirical distribution,

The normal curve of distribution has other properties, which make it of great value to statisticians. Let us consider the study shown above. We can ask some questions.

1 What is the chance that a particular score will fall below the mean?
2 Assuming our sample is representative, what is the likelihood that we will find people brighter than Azima if we choose them randomly?

The first question is easy to answer. As the shape is regular, and as it is exactly bisected by the mean, we can say that any particular score has a 50% chance of being below the mean. We can also say that we will have scores below the mean 50% of the time. This clearly links to the question of probability, which we deal with in the next section. We can say there is a 0.5 chance of getting a score below (or above) the mean.

We can know more than this. There is a relationship between the normal and standard deviation. You will remember that standard deviation is one of the measures of the *spread* of scores about the mean. The 'x' axis of the normal curve can be marked off in terms of standard deviation.

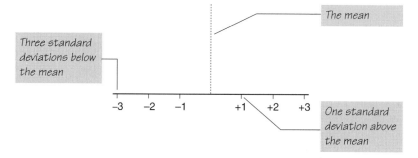

One feature of this curve is that about two-thirds of all the scores fall between −1 standard deviation and +1 standard deviation. We can therefore say that anyone chosen randomly has a 68% chance, more or less, of falling into that spread of scores. For IQ scores a standard deviation is about 15 IQ points. As the mean score is 100, we can say with some confidence that 68% of our sample will lie between an IQ of 85 and an IQ of 115. If we go as far as two standard deviations above and below the mean, we find that about 95% of the scores fall into that range. This leaves 5% outside that range. Beyond +2 standard deviations are IQ scores of 130 or more. Our chance of finding someone chosen randomly who scores over 130 is 2.5% – or half of 5%. (The other 2.5% is below −2 standard deviations, or below an IQ of 70.)

The main statistical properties of this important distribution are summarised below:

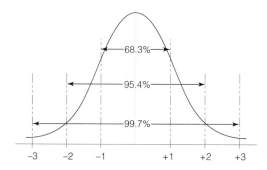

It is because of these properties of the normal curve that it can be used to enable us to estimate the likelihood that a given set of scores have come from a certain population. If we know the characteristics of a population, then we should be able to tell the chance that a particular sample (of scores) has come from that population. If we test the IQ scores of adults who have undertaken a course in meditation, and we find that the mean is distinctly *higher* than our general population, while the standard deviation is the same, we *may* conclude that the meditation has had some beneficial effect. We will be able to say, with considerable accuracy, what the chance is that this difference could have occurred by chance. Many of the statistical tests that you will use, especially the t-test, make use of distributions of scores related to the normal curve.

We asked above, what is the chance of finding people who score higher that Azima? She has an IQ score of 138. This is about 2.5 standard deviations above the mean. To find this out we use a table of what are known as *z-scores*. Z-scores are simply measures of standard deviation (1 z = 1 standard deviation). The table (to be found in most statistical texts) will tell the chance of a score falling beyond a particular standard deviation. In this case the chance is about 6 in 1,000. We will look next in more detail at the question of probability.

Probability

My father, an artist, once dropped his pencil. It bounced, and landed on its base, and there it stayed, point upwards. It looked impossible. Yet it happened. If he had spent years trying to do it, he probably would not have succeeded. The *chance* that it would happen was remote. But occasionally events that are very unlikely do occur. We will see below that this possibility can create problems for psychologists carrying out scientific experiments.

I once played a round of golf with a friend. At a particular part of the course he hit a cracking good drive from the tee. It disappeared on the green. We discovered he had made a hole-in-one. I suspect I will never see someone achieve that again. Yet, if we were to look at the statistics about golf players at international level, and review all the holes-in-one, it would be possible to work out the probability of such event for each time a player drives off at the tee. The equation is quite simple:

$$\text{Probability} = \frac{\text{Number of holes-in-one at this particular hole}}{\text{Number of drives made at this particular hole}}$$

We would expect the result to be a very small fraction.

> **Probability** can be defined as the *likelihood* that an event will happen in a given situation.

For certain events, the likelihood or *chance* of an event occurring can be worked out with great accuracy. If you toss a coin, what is the chance that it will come up heads? In everyday language we say the chance is fifty-fifty. In other words, we know that there is a one in two chance of getting a heads. If we toss the coin 100 times, then we would expect that about 50 of those times the coin will land head up.

Again, we can use our simple formula to work out the precise chance:

$$\text{Probability} = \frac{\text{the number of ways it can land heads (i.e. 1)}}{\text{the number of possible outcomes (i.e. 2)}}$$

In this case we can say

$$P = \tfrac{1}{2}$$

where P is the probability of achieving heads.

It could happen but is it likely?

In exploring the concept of probability, a group of psychology students all tossed coins at the same time. The first eight in the group each threw heads. This happened by chance. What our formula can tell us is whether such an event is, in fact, very unusual. For each student who threw a coin, the chance of getting a heads was one in two. Let us consider the first two students. Each can throw either a heads or a tails. The four possible outcomes are shown below:

Possible outcomes	1	2	3	4
Student 1	Heads	Heads	Tails	Tails
Student 2	Heads	Tails	Heads	Tails

Of the four possible outcomes, one is double heads, and three are not. The probability of achieving two heads with two students is therefore one in four.

$$P = \tfrac{1}{2} \times \tfrac{1}{2}$$

$$P = \tfrac{1}{4}$$

When we have eight students, then the chance of obtaining all heads is much less. We can calculate this as

$$P \text{ (all heads)} = \tfrac{1}{2} \times \tfrac{1}{2} \times \tfrac{1}{2} \times \tfrac{1}{2} \times \tfrac{1}{2} \times \tfrac{1}{2} \times \tfrac{1}{2} \times \tfrac{1}{2}$$

> This can also be written as $P = (\tfrac{1}{2})^8$

$$= \frac{1}{256}$$

The point about the story of the eight students who all threw heads is that it is very unlikely to happen, but it can happen, *by chance*. This would happen, on average, only once in every 256 attempts.

Psychologists are faced with the problem of deciding whether their results in an experiment have occurred because of some specific cause, or merely by chance.

A fictitious experiment
Researchers in the United States have discovered that listening to Mozart improves IQ scores temporarily. A psychologist decides to test the impact of Mozart's music on problem solving. He invites 20 students to participate in an experiment. He divides the group randomly into two groups of 10. The first group hears 15 minutes of Mozart. The second group sit in silence for 15 minutes. Both are then given some problems to solve. The scores achieved are as follows:

	Mozart group		Silence group
P1	84	P11	76
P2	75	P12	56
P3	93	P13	63
P4	86	P14	86
P5	74	P15	65
P6	63	P16	74
P7	80	P17	54
P8	89	P18	81
P9	77	P19	93
P10	91	P20	69
Total	812		717
Mean	81.2		71.7

This would seem to suggest that listening to Mozart improves the ability of students to solve problems. But does it? The researcher is always faces with the question 'Could these results have occurred by chance?'.

What we can see from studying the figures is that the 'Mozart' group have scored, on average, 15.8 more than the 'silence' group, on the intelligence test. We can also compare the scores of each of the pairs of participants in each group, as they were randomly allocated.

	Mozart group		Silence group	Sign of difference
P1	84	P11	76	+
P2	75	P12	56	+
P3	93	P13	63	+
P4	86	P14	86	0
P5	74	P15	65	+
P6	63	P16	74	−
P7	80	P17	54	+
P8	89	P18	81	+
P9	77	P19	93	−
P10	91	P20	69	+

The sign column indicates where the 'Mozart' group score higher than the 'silence' group.

We can treat these scores (in terms of + and −) in the same way that we would treat tossing a coin, and getting heads and tails. Where the 'Mozart' participant scores higher, we can call that a 'heads'; where the 'silence' participant scores higher we can call that a 'tails'. An equal score, as with participants P4 and P14, will be ignored.

If we toss a coin nine times, we would generally expect to get 4 or 5 heads and 4 or 5 tails. What is the chance that we would get 1 tails and 8 heads? There are 9 different ways; this is one:

Throw	1	2	3	4	5	6	7	8	9
	H	H	H	H	H	H	H	H	
									T

The tails T could occur in any of the nine positions. The chance of this can be calculated. The formula is:

$$p = 9 \times (1/2)^9$$

$$p = 9 \times 1/512$$

$$p = 0.018$$

This means that there is a 1.8 chance in 100 that this result will occur by chance.

We can apply these findings to our music experiment. We can conclude that if only chance was operating, then if we carried out the experiment 100 times, we would expect our result to occur entirely fortuitously, slightly less than two times. So we can say with some confidence that our result is very likely to have been caused by the playing of the music. We will see later that all our statistical tests provide us with a number that can indicate the probability that our result has occurred by chance. This will also indicate how significant our results are.

Probability and significance

The lower the likelihood that something has occurred by chance, the more *significant* it is. If the result of an experiment cannot easily be explained as accidental, then it is possible to conclude that the independent variable was affecting the outcome. So, a very low probability or chance means a very high significance. It means that we can be very confident that our result is of consequence. In our example, the probability of our outcome occurring by chance is $P = .018$. This also is a numerical statement of the significance level.

We are faced with a question at this point. How significant do results have to be in order for us to be confident that they have not occurred by chance? This is a matter of judgement. There is always a risk that we will make a mistake in coming to this judgement. Generally, a greater chance than 1 in 20 is considered too high. If psychologists conduct an experiment and their results could have occurred by chance, say 1 time in 18, then this will *not* be considered significant. A chance of 5%, or 1 in 20, is, *by convention*, considered to be the highest level of chance that is acceptable.

A psychologist carrying out an investigation will need to decide *before* he or she starts interpreting the data what level of significance will be acceptable. To choose a higher probability level (and thus a lower level of significance) means it is easier to accept the experimental hypothesis. To apply a stricter level will make it less easy to accept the experimental hypothesis. However, it will mean that if that level is achieved, then the psychologist can have greater confidence in the result. Whatever choice is made, there is a chance of making a mistake. We will explore this problem next.

Sampling

When psychologists carry out research they are interested in what generalisations they can make about behaviour. How far do their discoveries in relation to a particular sample apply to the population as a whole? If their sample is too restrictive, too small or too particular, then it may not be possible to make any meaningful generalisations. How a sample is chosen is therefore of considerable importance. The main considerations are:

- How representative is it?
- How far can generalisations be made?

We need first to clarify certain terms. 'The population' could mean all the human beings or all the rats that are potentially available for study. In fact it is usually more restricted than this. The population will be the total group that you are interested in studying; it might be a species of bee or it might be children of a given age group living in a British city. The 'sample' is the actual group that is studied. We need to consider the relationship between the two.

> Population: the set or group that is being studied; the group about which generalisations will be made. This can be called the 'target population'.

The selection of the sample is going to be crucial in determining how representative it is. The group from whom the sample is selected is called 'the sampling frame'.

> Sampling frame: the list, or the actual group from which participants are actually chosen.

You select some people to be in an experiment. You choose them from people who happen to be studying in the college library. Your sampling frame is then students who are in the college library at that particular time. You will need to consider how far they are representative of your *target population*, the group you are actually interested in.

> Sample: the group actually selected to be participants. The group who are directly studied.

How you make your selection from your sampling frame will determine how representative your sample is of the sampling frame. If you just choose friends and acquaintances, then it may not be representative at all. If you take every tenth person, then it may be much more representative.

We can summarise with a diagram:

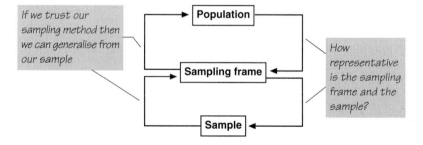

83

Selecting a sample

Many students will not be in a position really to establish a proper sampling frame for the work that they do. When you select your sample from other classmates, or friends and relations, then the sample is an '**opportunity sample**'. You will have to make a judgement about how far you can generalise and what sort of target population they represent.

Random samples

A random sample means that everyone in the sampling frame has an equal chance of being chosen. Taking every nth name from a list is a good example of a random selection. Choosing from a numbered list, with random numbers, or putting all names into a hat and selecting a number are other methods. Do *not* call an opportunity sample 'random'. It isn't. When you are carrying out an independent measures design, and you divide your group into two, it is very important that this is done randomly.

Quota samples

This is when you choose a number of participants who fit into various categories: for example, ten over the age of 40 and ten below the age of 20. When you reach your quota, then you do not select any more in that category.

Problems, guessing and proof

A psychologist, like any scientist, starts his or her exploration on the basis of a problem that confronts them. Pavlov, the famous Russian scientist, noticed that his dogs salivated when his assistants came in with their food dish. They were responding to sounds the assistant made or to the sight of the dish. He realised that here was a problem to be explained. To find the possible cause he would need some idea about why dogs might salivate when they saw something that was not in itself edible. This idea would derive from a **theory**. At this stage his theory would have been very sketchy. In the course of time it became elaborated into the famous proposition of Classical Conditioning.

> **Theory** – a system of ideas that provides an explanation for why something is the way it is or why it has developed the way it has. A theory is, in essence, a model of how something is, how it works or what has caused it.

Why does the Muller-Lyer illusion work? How does memory operate? What is the cause of schizophrenia? Are women more effective in management than men? Each of these questions is a problem that confronts psychologists. To approach the question an initial 'working model' is used. For the Muller-Lyer illusion, Richard Gregory

thought perhaps it was the effect of being raised in an environment consisting of straight lines and corners, in houses. With regard to memory, Atkinson and Shiffrin came up with the idea that there might be two different stores, one for the short-term memory and one for the long term. In each case their theories provided models that could be tested.

A proposition derived from a theory or model is an **hypothesis**. An hypothesis will be used by a scientist to help focus their research. To be scientiflc it must be *testable*.

> **Hypothesis** – a conjecture or proposition that can be tested. It originates from a theory and is usually more specific than a theory or model. To be truly scientific it should be *falsifiable*. Two types of hypothesis are used. The **Experimental** or **Alternate Hypothesis** is a proposition that one variable will have a measurable effect on another variable, or that they will be related in a measurable way. The **Null Hypothesis** suggests that there will be no significant relationship between variables.

Karl Popper, the eminent philosopher of science, established that it was not really possible to *prove* anything was true. His classic example was that it was not possible to prove that 'all swans are white'. However many swans you observe, it is always possible that the next swan that is discovered could be black. The null hypothesis, or negative proposition, that 'no swans are white', could easily be disproved. If all the many swans observed so far are white then there is a high *probability* that subsequent swans will be white.

The laws of science, seen from this point of view, are not completely certain. They are usually statements of very high probability. For long-established laws we do not expect them to be suddenly refuted or disproved. But there is always the possibility that they could be. For this reason we do not suggest, as psychologists, that we have 'proved the experimental hypothesis'. It is preferable to say we 'accept it' or 'support it'. After all, in the nineteenth century it was 'proved' that men were more intelligent than women, because women demonstrably had smaller brains. When research was published asserting this, it was hardly challenged. This was because it was obvious to the scientific community (nearly entirely men) that it was true. Only towards the end of the century was the proposition soundly refuted. As we have already seen, the results of our experiments lead us to be able to state the probability that a particular hypothesis is acceptable or is false. There is always the possibility that we are in error. This brings us back to the issue of probability and significance levels.

If we wish to minimise the possibility that we will support the experimental hypothesis, when it is in fact untrue, then we will adopt a more stringent probability level. We might do this if we wished to be sure that the results of a personality test used in the selection of employees for a large firm had not occurred by chance. We would like to be very confident that our results could be trusted, both for the success of the firm and also to know that applicants were being treated fairly. We would probably choose the 1% level and reduce our risk of error to 1 in 100 or less.

So why don't psychologists always choose a very stringent level of probability and reduce the chance of accepting a false experimental hypothesis? The reason is that, if they are too strict, then they may reject an experimental hypothesis that is actually true. The trend may be in the data, but not sufficient to reach a confidence level of $p \leqslant 0.01$

Type I and Type II error

There are two types of error that a psychologist might make. One is to accept an experimental hypothesis that is in fact false. The other is to reject an hypothesis that is in reality true. (As we have just seen, it is not possible ever to know whether we have made either of these errors, *with complete certainty*.) To understand the risk that we take as psychologists, we need to consider the two types of probability score that concern us. The first is the *confidence level* that we choose prior to undertaking our investigation. This is the level of probability that we wish to achieve to enable us to reject the null hypothesis and support the experimental hypothesis. The second level of probability is related to our *test result*. This is the probability that our results have occurred by chance. If this second probability is smaller than the confidence level we selected prior to undertaking our study, then we support the experimental hypothesis. If it is not, then we assume that the null hypothesis is probably true. An example will help explain:

> Mozart revisited: we select, by convention, a confidence level of 5% or 0.05. We are testing the proposition that listening to Mozart's music temporarily produces higher IQ scores. We achieve, as can be seen in the previous section, a test statistic with a probability of 0.018. This means that we can support our experimental hypothesis. However, there is a 1.8% chance that we have accepted an experimental hypothesis that is in fact wrong. This would be a **Type I error**. If, to avoid this, we decide to have a stricter confidence level to achieve, and set it at 0.01, then we would have to reject the experimental hypothesis. (0.018 is bigger than 0.01.) We would accept the null hypothesis. If the null hypothesis was *not* actually true, then we would have made a **Type II error**.

These two risks can be summed up in the following diagram:

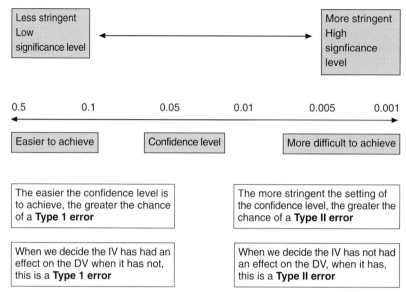

Note: the IV is the Independent Variable, the DV is the Dependent Variable. These terms are defined on page 88.

Returning to our example of the Mozart music experiment, we are able to accept that listening to the music had an effect on the IQ scores achieved. Yet we cannot say that this is true, with absolute certitude. All we can say is, that on these results, we have only 1.8 chances in 100 of being wrong. Overall, we can conclude that our theory of intelligence may need to take account of the effect of baroque music. We have added a little to our store of knowledge about the problem of what influences intelligence.

Proof

As scientists, psychologists are trying to establish what the truth is about human and animal behaviour. As we have already seen, they cannot be completely certain of any of their discoveries. They can know the probability that they are right. We have looked at their dilemma in some detail in our discussion of Type I and Type II error.

A psychologist is on firm ground when describing their findings. With descriptive statistics, which we looked on pages 62–74, we can be quite certain about the characteristics of our sample. When we wish to interpret our data, and to generalise from it, then we find we cannot be so sure. An analogy will help.

Weather announcers, on television, can describe with great certainty what the weather was like the previous day. The level of rainfall, the hours of sunshine and the air pressure, can be known precisely. When they come to prediction they are less successful. They

87

are having to infer about the future from findings that have happened in the past.

The psychologist is in a comparable position. They have to infer from their sample what the characteristics are of their target population. Taking a specific example, a sample of students at a particular college take an IQ test. It may be possible to infer from the results something about the IQ profile of the students as a whole. The type of statistics used is called **inferential statistics**. They always involve probabilities, and not certainties. Inferential statistics are a way of assessing the likelihood that an hypothesis is correct. We need to look a little more closely at what this means.

Causality

Scientific research is concerned with finding out relationships between variables. If we irradiate food (irradiation is one variable) will the food last longer? (How long it lasts is another variable.) Some variables can be manipulated; this means the experimenter can change them by degrees. For example, we can investigate the effect of numbers of people on the likelihood that a specific participant will help another, who is apparently in distress. The numbers of people (ranging from one to several) is the variable that is manipulated. The readiness to help, measured by whether they help or not, or how long it takes them to offer help, is the outcome.

The variable that we can manipulate directly is called the **independent variable**. The measured outcome is called the **dependent variable**. We are assuming, usually from the theory that we are using, that there is a *causal* relationship between the two. In other words, our investigations rest on the assumption that the change in the independent variable directly causes an effect on the dependent variable.

> The independent variable (IV) is the variable that is expected to produce a change in another variable. By manipulating this variable, the experimenter sees if a change is produced in the dependent variable.

For example, in an experiment on memory, the independent variable may be whether the group has been advised to make mental images of the words given in the list or not. The dependent variable is the number of words remembered under the two conditions. Statistics can be used to infer whether the outcome suggests that there is a causal relationship between using imagery and better memory for words.

> The dependent variable (DV) is the variable that is affrected, or may be affected, by the IV.

Some variables are categories that cannot be manipulated. When we compare the results in a test taken by males and females, we cannot manipulate the sex. We can only compare the outcome from the male group and contrast that to the female group. Being male or female, in itself, cannot be assumed to be the cause. It may be some other factor associated with masculinity and femininity that is producing the result. For example, socialisation experiences of both sexes may be different. This may be the actual cause. For this reason, when we carry out an experiment of this kind, it is called a *non-causal* design. We will have more to say about this in the next section.

Design

Imagine an experiment where the effect of noise levels on a maths test was being investigated. Here the IV, noise level, can be directly manipulated. With careful control, the effect of this manipulation on the DV, performance in the test, can be measured. Here the change in the IV is apparently the direct cause of the change in the DV. The design is causal.

In another experiment, the performance of females on a perception task is compared with that of males. The IV here is gender. However, we cannot be sure that any measured differences on the perception task between the two groups were caused by biological differences. The cause might be some other factor, like socialisation. Strictly, we have to say that the experimenter cannot directly manipulate the IV and so the design is really non-causal.

Both of these designs are tests of differences between groups or conditions. We are looking at how a change in conditions produces a change in some other factor. There are three fundamental designs: repeated measures, matched groups and independent measures.

Repeated measures   If an experiment uses the *same* group of subjects under different conditions, then this is an example of a *repeated measures* design. With this type of design, each subject acts as their own control because any extraneous variables, like how tired they are, what they have eaten, their physical or mental skills etc., can be expected to be the same under both conditions.

> **Repeated measures**: here one group carries out the same task under two different conditions. This can also be called within-groups related design.
>
> **Matched groups**: here two groups are matched as carefully as possible in pairs. They are allocated randomly to one or other groups. Each group carries out the task under a different condition of the IV. This can also be called a matched-pairs related design.
>
> **Independent measures**: here subjects are randomly allocated to one of two groups. This can also be called a between-groups unrelated design.

Matched groups   Where a repeated measures design is not possible, because performing under one condition of the IV would influence performance under the other condition (e.g. in a problem-solving experiment, where a clue is given), a *matched pairs* design may be used. Here subjects are matched in pairs that are as similar as possible for all relevant characteristics. They are then each allocated to different groups. The groups can then be treated as though they were repeated measures, for statistical purposes.

There is another type of non-causal design. This is the correlation, where the degree of relationship or association between two characteristics is being measured. Often a correlation will assess the degree of association of two characteristics in the same individuals. For example, rating people for introversion-extroversion and also for prejudice.

Correlational designs usually use 'repeated measures' in terms of the way they are conducted. Sometimes they will require matching groups. However, it must be remembered they are not testing for differences but for relationships, and they are not causal.

Independent measures It is difficult and time consuming to try and set up an experiment with matched groups, and not all experiments can be repeated measures. Many use two groups, not necessarily of equal numbers, who experience the different conditions of the experiment. This type of design is *independent measures*. Allocation to the two groups should be as random as possible, nevertheless, to avoid errors creeping in.

When we have designed and carried out our experiment, we then have to assess from our data whether there is a strong likelihood that there is a causal connection between the variables. To do that we use statistical tests. We turn to these next.

Statistical tests

Choosing statistics for your study

In order to do this you will need to decide or establish answers to the following:

1 Is your study an **experiment** or an **observation**?

While an observation needs to be systematic, with an hypothesis, it will not be structured, with a clear design and manipulation of the independent variable, as in an experiment.

2 If it is an experiment what is the **design**?

Is it **one-group/matched groups** involving **repeated measures** or is it **two groups** involving **independent measures**?
Or
is it a **non-causal** design, investigation **association** or **correlation**?

3 Is the **hypothesis** you are using **one-tailed** or **two-tailed**?

If you are predicting that the independent variable will affect the dependent variable in a particular way (e.g., specifying 'greater' or 'lesser'), then it is a **one-tailed hypothesis**. Otherwise it is **two-tailed**.

4 What level of **data** has your experiment produced?

Nominal – names or classification into categories e.g., smokers, non-smokers.
Ordinal – data that can be put in *rank order* e.g., judgements of attractiveness.
Interval – where the units of measurement are of *equal dimension* e.g., IQ scores
Ratio – the same as interval data but with an '*absolute zero*' e.g., time.

5 Are the data suitable for a **parametric** test?

To be suitable the data must:
– be at least **interval** status
– be **normally** distributed
– have very similar **variance**

6 What **descriptive** statistics are appropriate?

Raw data in a report need to be presented in an organised form:
– bar charts, pie charts, graphs, scattergrams; tables of data;
– measures of central tendency, the **mean, median** and **mode;**
– measures of dispersion, the **variance, standard deviation, range**.

7 What **inferential** statistics can be used (if any)?

Choice of **parametric** or **non-parametric** tests.

8 What **level of significance** has been chosen?

What probability level is appropriate for the experiment?

These criteria can now be applied to the flow chart below to decide which statistics test is appropriate for the experiment.

Choosing the statistical test

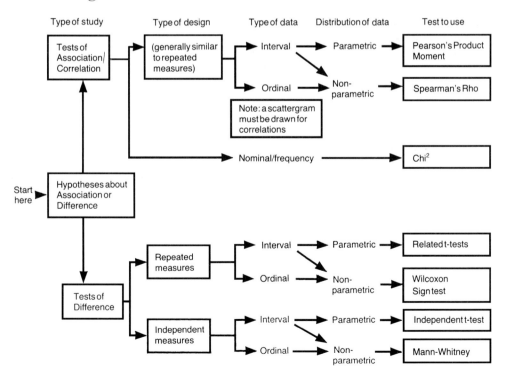

The statistical tests

In this section we will look at the main inferential statistical tests that you are likely to use. We will consider what the appropriate test is for the data you have collected. The main steps will be presented along with a worked example. The strengths and weaknesses of the tests will be summarised.

First we will look at *tests of association*. These are tests which measure the strength of relationship between data in our samples:

- Chi^2 test
- Tests of correlation

Then we will consider *tests of difference*. These tests measure the degree to which samples differ from each other. These we will divide into two groups:

1 Tests of difference where the design is repeated measures or matched groups; here data are in pairs.

- Sign test
- Wilcoxon signed-rank test
- Related t-test

2 Tests of difference where the design is independent measures; here data are *not paired*.

- Mann-Whitney U test
- Independent t-test

Using statistical tables

All the tables in this section work in a similar way, except for the Mann-Whitney test.

Table page 95 adapted from A. Edwards and R. Talbot *The Hard-Pressed Researcher* Longman 1994. With kind permission of the authors and publishers.

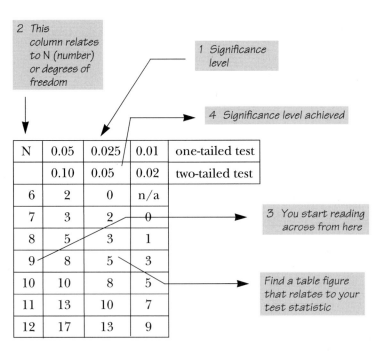

N	0.05	0.025	0.01	one-tailed test
	0.10	0.05	0.02	two-tailed test
6	2	0	n/a
7	3	2	0
8	5	3	1
9	8	5	3
10	10	8	5
11	13	10	7
12	17	13	9

2 *This column relates to N (number) or degrees of freedom*

1 *Significance level*

4 *Significance level achieved*

3 *You start reading across from here*

Find a table figure that relates to your test statistic

Using this table

Read across from N (the number of paired scores).
Look for a value on the table that is **equal to or greater than** the value of . . .

5 *Follow these instructions as appropriate*

1 The top of the table gives the significance levels. These are for a one-tailed test (on the top) and a two-tailed test (underneath). If you are not sure which you are testing, look at your hypothesis. If you predict a specific *direction* to your outcome, it is *one*-tailed. If you predict a significant difference but not in a given direction, it is *two*-tailed.

2 The upper left-hand corner relates either to the number of subjects (or pairs of subjects, N) or to degrees of freedom. You read down this column to the relevant part of the table.

3 You then read across till you find the number on the table that relates to your test statistic. You will have to follow the instructions given *under* the table to find the correct figure. Sometimes you will look for a figure greater than your test statistic, sometimes for one that is smaller.

4 When you have found the relevant number you look up that column to the significance level achieved, for a one- or two-tailed test, as appropriate. This is your level of significance or the probability that your result happened by chance. A level of 0.05 or *lower* is considered statistically significant.

5 Carefully read the instructions under the table.

The chi² test: 2×2

When to use the test

Type of test	*Test of association.*
Type of design	*Unrelated design – your data will be in distinct categories.*
Type of data	*Nominal – recorded as frequencies.*
Other requirements	*The data must be in terms of actual numbers (frequencies) and not percentages.*
	An item in a cell must be independent of items in other cells.
	Expected frequencies should not fall below five.

What happens in the test

The data will be in cells. For example, these might be *males who smoke, females who smoke, males who do not smoke* and *females who do not smoke.* Each participant would fit into only one category or cell. In the test the actual frequency is compared to the expected frequency. This means that the actual distribution of data is compared to what might be expected if there was no association or connectedness between the two variables being considered, in this case *sex* and *smoking.* If there were, say 20 men and 30 women in the survey, we might expect the distribution to be like this:

	Men	Women	Total
Smokers	10	15	25
Non-smokers	10	15	25
Total	20	30	50

This is the distribution of expected frequencies.

If there *is* an association between the sex of the participant and smoking, then we would expect the actual distribution of scores to be different. For example:

	Men	Women	Total
Smokers	14	11	25
Non-smokers	6	19	25
Total	20	30	50

In the test we will be looking at how big the difference is between the *actual frequencies* and the *expected frequencies.* An 'eyeball' test on the data suggests that males smoke more than females, at least in this sample of 50 people. We would have to carry out the test to see if the degree of association between sex and smoking was significant.

Calculation of the chi² test

| | **Example** |

Step 1

Draw up a table of the observed frequencies (O). Label the cells (A, B, C and D). Work out the row totals and the column totals. These should both add together to the grand total (T). Then draw up a *contingency* table. This will have rows and columns of data. Leave plenty of space on the table.

Step 1

	Men	**Women**	**Total**
Smokers	A 14	B 11	25
Non-smokers	C 6	D 19	25
Total	20	30	50

Contingency Table

Cell	O	E	$|O-E|$
A			
B			
C			
D			

Note: $|O-E|$ means 'subtract smaller from larger'

Step 2

Calculate the expected frequencies (E). For each cell use the formula:

$$E = \frac{\text{row total} \times \text{column total}}{\text{grand total } (T)}$$

Step 2

For Cell A $\quad E = \dfrac{25 \times 20}{50} \quad E = 10$

For Cell B $\quad E = \dfrac{25 \times 30}{50} \quad E = 15$

For Cell C $\quad E = \dfrac{25 \times 20}{50} \quad E = 10$

For Cell D $\quad E = \dfrac{25 \times 30}{50} \quad E = 15$

Step 3

For each cell find the difference between the expected frequency (E) and the observed frequency (O); subtract the smaller from the larger.

Step 3

Cell A	$14 - 10 = 4$
Cell B	$15 - 11 = 4$
Cell C	$10 - 6 = 4$
Cell D	$19 - 15 = 4$

Cell	**O**	**E**	**$|O - E|$**
A	14	10	4
B	11	15	4
C	6	10	4
D	19	15	4

Step 4

For each cell square the results from Step 3 and divide by the expected frequency (E) for that cell.

Note: Some texts suggest a manipulation called Yates' Correction is needed for small numbers, when doing a chi^2 test. Generally, mathematicians now believe this is unnecessary.

Step 4

Cell A $\quad \dfrac{4^2}{10} = 1.6$

Cell B $\quad \dfrac{4^2}{15} = 1.067$

Cell C $\quad \dfrac{4^2}{10} = 1.6$

Cell D $\quad \dfrac{4^2}{15} = 1.067$

Step 5

Add together the outcomes of Step 4. This is the value of chi^2.

Step 5

$1.6 + 1.067 + 1.6 + 1.067 = 5.334$
$\chi^2 = 5.334$

Step 6

Work out the *degrees of freedom* (*df*). Calculated by multiplying the number of rows less 1 by the number of columns less 1.

Step 6

$df = (2-1) \times (2-1) = 1$

Step 7

Use the table of critical values of chi^2 to see degree of significance of the outcome.

Step 7

Look at the first Statistical Table (**ST1**) on page 100.

	0.025 0.05	0.005 0.01	0.0005 0.001
df 1 2	3.84 5.99	6.64 9.21	10.83 13.82

If the prediction *before* we did the survey of smoking was that men would smoke more than women, then the hypothesis would be *one-tailed*.

The χ^2 statistic of 5.334 is greater than the table value of 3.84 at *df* = 1; it is less than the value 6.64 at *df* = 1. Looking up the column from the value 3.84, we find the level of significance is 0.025 for a one-tailed test. We can conclude:
$p < 0.025$

Table ST1 Critical values of χ^2

Degrees of freedom	Levels of significance			
	0.025	0.005	0.0005	one-tailed list
	0.05	0.01	0.001	two-tailed list
1	3.84	6.64	10.83	
2	5.99	9.21	13.82	
3	7.82	11.34	16.27	
4	9.49	13.28	18.46	
5	11.07	15.09	20.52	
6	12.59	16.81	22.46	
7	14.07	18.48	24.32	
8	15.51	20.09	26.12	
9	16.92	21.67	27.88	
10	18.31	23.21	29.59	
11	19.68	24.72	31.26	
12	21.03	26.22	32.91	
13	22.36	27.69	34.53	
14	23.68	29.14	36.12	
15	25.00	30.58	37.70	
16	26.3	32.0	39.25	
17	27.6	33.4	40.79	
18	28.9	34.8	42.31	
19	30.1	36.2	43.82	
20	31.4	37.6	45.32	

(Adapted from Table IV, R. A. Fisher and F. Yates, *Statistical Tables for Biological, Agricultural and Medical Research* 6th edn, Oliver & Boyd 1963.)

Using this table

Read across from the relevent degree of freedom. Look for a value on the table that is **equal to or greater than** the value of χ^2. Look above that figure, to the top of the table, to see the level of significance achieved. Values for a two-tailed test are given below values for a one-tailed test.

The chi^2 test: other contingency groupings

We have just considered the chi^2 test for two samples and two categories (males and females, smoking and non-smoking). There are other situations in which a chi^2 test is appropriate. The first is when there is only **one** sample and **two** categories. This produces a 1 × 2 table. The second is where there is **one** sample and **several** categories. The third is **more than one sample** and **several** categories.

One sample and two categories

The method of calculating the value of χ^2 is the same as that shown for a 2×2 contingency table. The same requirements (of independence of data, and expected frequencies not falling below 5) apply. There will be 1 degree of freedom.

Example

You are researching the preference people have for a particular brand of cola. You give 30 people a taste test. They state their preference. Is the result significant?

	Diet cola	Standard cola	Total
Participants	8	22	30

Following the same procedure given above, you will find the expected frequency for each cell is 15. Steps 4 to 6 will give a result for χ^2 of **6.53**. This means your result is significant for a two-tailed test at $p < 0.05$. Standard cola is preferred by significantly more people.

One sample and several categories

This situation is also known as a test of 'goodness of fit'.

When to use the test

Type of test	*Test of association.*
Type of design	*Unrelated design – your data will be in distinct categories.*
Type of data	*Nominal – recorded as frequencies.*
Other requirements	*The data must be in terms of actual numbers (frequencies) and not percentages.*
	An item in a cell must be independent of items in other cells.
	Yates' correction need not be applied.

Example

In supermarkets, you will have seen magazines sold at the counter. These are aimed at people buying on impulse. If the cover is 'right' then many more people will buy one. You want to test people's preference for various covers for women's magazines. Your sample is 40 females, between the ages of 20 and 40. You have six magazines. You ask each participant to choose the cover they like best.

Magazine	1	2	3	4	5	6	Total
Female participants	4	1	5	18	10	2	40

Calculations

Step 1

Draw up a contingency table.

Categories	O	E	O−E	(O−E)²	$\frac{(O-E)^2}{E}$
1					
2					
3					
etc.					
Sum					

O = Observed frequency
E = Expected frequency

Step 2

Fill in the table with your results, putting in the observed frequencies (O) and the expected frequencies (E). E is calculated by dividing the total frequencies by the number of categories. Complete the table.

Step 3

Add together the results of your final column

to give you the sum of $\dfrac{(O-E)^2}{E}$

The result is the value for χ^2

Step 4

For this type of test degrees of freedom will be the number of categories -1.

Step 5

Look up your result on Table ST1. Read across from the degree of freedom to the score that is equal to or smaller than your statistic for χ^2. Look up that column to find the significance level.

Example

Steps 1–3

Magazines	O	E	O−E	(O−E)²	$\frac{(O-E)^2}{E}$
1	4	6.67	2.67	7.11	1.07
2	1	6.67	5.67	32.11	4.82
3	5	6.67	1.67	2.78	0.42
4	18	6.67	11.33	128.44	19.27
5	10	6.67	3.33	11.11	1.67
6	2	6.67	4.67	21.78	3.27
Sum					30.5

Step 4

$df = 6-1$
$df = 5$

Step 5

A result of $\chi^2 = 30.5$ is bigger than the critical value of 20.52 on Table ST1 for 5 degrees of freedom. It achieves a significance level of at least $p < 0.001$ for a two-tailed test.

Ranking

Some statistical tests require data to be ranked. This is a simple process if you keep your wits about you. It is best to write out properly the figures you wish to rank and not to try to do the process in your head, or on a scrap of paper.

Calculations

Example

A psychologist has developed a test for self-esteem. The participants receive scores of 0–10, where 10 is high self-esteem.

Step 1

Use a table with three columns to work out your ranks.

Scores in size order	Scores numbered	Ranks
	1	
	2	
	3	
	4	
	etc.	

Write out all the scores you want to rank, from smallest to largest. If values occur more than once (repetitions) you include all of them.

Step 2

Next to these, write figures from one to *n*, where *n* is the total number of scores you are ranking.

Step 3

In the final column put the ranks. If all the scores are different, then the ranks will be the same as the numbering. A single score has the same rank as its number. If there are tied scores, then the average *number* is taken. An odd number of scores is ranked as the mid-most number. An even number of scores is ranked as half-way between the two middle numbers.

Steps 1–3

Score	N°	Rank
4	1	3
4	2	3
4	3	3
4	4	3
4	5	3
5	6	7.5
5	7	7.5
5	8	7.5
5	9	7.5
6	10	10
7	11	12.5
7	12	12.5
7	13	12.5
7	14	12.5
8	15	17
8	16	17
8	17	17
8	18	17
8	19	17
9	20	20

There are five scores of 4; the middle is 3 and each receives a value of 3.

There are four scores of 5; the middle is half-way between 7 and 8. The rank is 7.5

Where there is only one value, the rank is the same as the numerical position.

Correlation

When to use the test

Type of test   *Test of association.*
Type of design   *The design will involve repeated measures in some form.*
Type of data   *Ordinal or interval data.*
Other requirements   *Scores must be in pairs.*
                        There must be good reason to believe the scores are related in some way.

What happens in the test

A correlation is looking for the nature of the **relationship** between pairs of scores. We can expect that there should be a clear relationship between people's height and the length of their feet. The taller they are the longer their feet should be. Their height does not *cause* their feet to grow longer, but both are related to the genetic (and environmental) factors that determine body size. A test of correlation is measuring the strength of that relationship.

Sometimes we may expect a correlation to be measuring a *causal relationship*. We may assume that one of the variables directly causes the other. All other things being equal, length of time spent revising should correlate with scores achieved on a test. However, a correlation between pairs of scores does not, in itself, *prove* a relationship. There may well be a correlation between the number of active coal mines in Great Britain over the last ten years and achievement at GCSE. The fewer the mines operative the better the GCSE scores. The decline in mining has run in parallel with the improvement in GCSE scores. There is no reason to believe there is any particular causal link between these two things.

Generally your test scores will be produced by participants being measured for two variables (e.g., attitude to violence in films and the number of violent films seen in the last three months). Sometimes the scores may be generated by participants in relation to something else. Research has shown that couples who marry often are similar in terms of how attractive they are. A very attractive man will tend to marry an attractive woman. This can be tested by having participants measure the level of attractiveness of pictures of brides and (separately) pictures of grooms. The prediction is that there will be a *positive* correlation between these scores (i.e., the more attractive the bride, the more attractive the groom). The mean scores of attractiveness for each picture is then calculated.

Mean scores for attractiveness out of ten (10 = very attractive)

	Bride	**Groom**
Couple 1	5.9	7.1
Couple 2	9.3	8.4
Couple 3	3.6	2.3
Couple 4	6.4	6.2
Couple 5	2.2	1.9
Couple 6	8.4	7.2

Plotting a scattergram

The first step in investigating a correlation is to plot a **scattergram**.

Calculations	Examples
Step 1	**Step 1**
Draw up a table of data, with each pair of scores in adjacent columns.	See above – table of scores for bride and groom

Case	First variable	Second variable
1		
2		
3		
etc.		

Step 2

Plot a scattergram, using one variable as the '*x' axis* and one as the '*y' axis*. Remember to label the axes. (The 'x' axis is *horizontal* the 'y' axis is *vertical*.)

Step 2

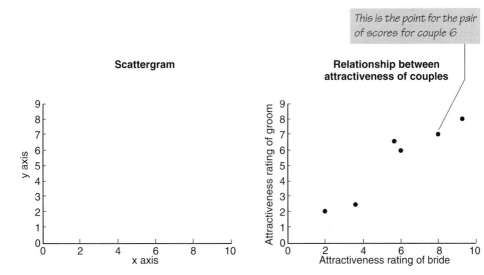

This is the point for the pair of scores for couple 6

Scattergram

Relationship between attractiveness of couples

What does a scattergram show?

A scattergram indicates the relationship between variables. Visually, it gives an indication of the strength of that relationship. If all the data fall on a straight line then the following relationships are indicated.

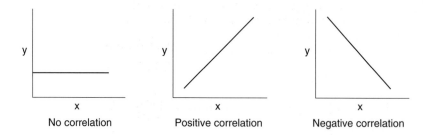

No correlation Positive correlation Negative correlation

When plotting a scattergram, you will be looking for how far they appear to be producing a straight line indicating a positive or negative correlation. (Can you see why the first example given above is *no correlation*? The reason is that the variable on the 'y' axis does not alter at all with variation on the 'x' axis. Hence there is no relationship.) A scattergram gives a pattern of dots that will tend towards a negative or positive correlation. Or it may show no correlation at all.

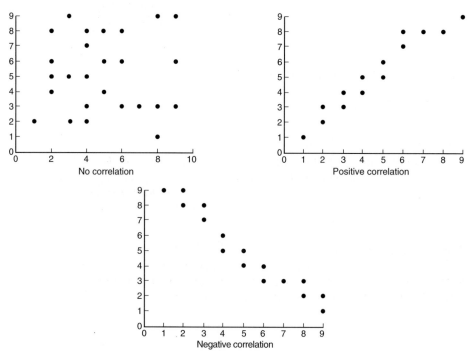

The correlation coefficient

What does the correlation coefficient mean?

The correlation coefficient represents the amount of relationship that is found between the two variables. A perfect positive relationship is expressed by the number +1. A perfect negative relationship is expressed by the number −1. If there is no relationship at all, then the number will be 0. In diagrammatic form it would look like this:

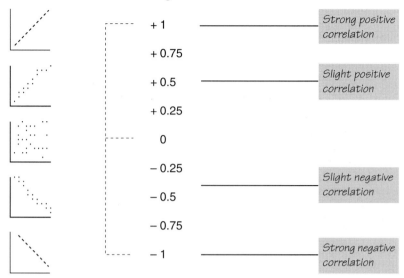

+ 1		Strong positive correlation
+ 0.75		
+ 0.5		Slight positive correlation
+ 0.25		
0		
− 0.25		
− 0.5		Slight negative correlation
− 0.75		
− 1		Strong negative correlation

Calculating Spearman's rho

When to use the test

Additional requirements

Type of data   *Ordinal data.*

Other requirements   *If the scattergram shows the data are slightly curved, this test can be used.*
Data are not parametric (i.e. interval measures, fitting normal curve of distribution and of similar variance).

What happens in the test
The paired data are compared using *ranks*. The test shows how closely the ranks of each pair of scores are related to one another. Ranks are used because the data are not parametric.

Table for Spearman's rho

Cases	Score A	Score B	Rank A (R_A)	Rank B (R_B)	Difference d	d^2
P1						
P2						
P3						
etc.						
$N=$						$\Sigma d^2 =$

Cases refers to paired scores from participants or measurements taken.

Calculations

Step 1

Draw up a table for your data. See table above.
Score A is the first variable in the pair;
Score B is the second variable.
Rank $A(R_A)$ are the ranks for variable A.
Rank B (R_B) are the ranks for variable B.
Difference d is the outcome of $R_A - R_B$
d^2 is the square of the difference d.

Step 2

Rank the scores for variable A.
(See how to calculate ranks, above, on page 103.)

Step 3

Rank scores for variable B.

Step 4

Subtract R_B from R_A to get d.

Step 5

Square d to get d^2

Step 6

Add up all the d^2 to get the Σd^2
(where Σ = 'sum of')

Step 7

Calculate N (where N is the number of paired scores).

Example

Steps 1–6

Fill in table, as shown below.
We will use the data for mean scores of attractiveness, given above on page 104.

Cases	Score A	Score B	Rank A (R_A)	Rank B (R_B)	d	d
1	5.9	7.1	3	4	−1	1
2	9.3	8.4	6	6	0	0
3	3.6	2.3	2	2	0	0
4	6.4	6.2	4	3	1	1
5	2.2	1.9	1	1	0	0
6	8.4	7.2	5	5	0	0
$N = 6$						Σd^2

Step 7

$N = 6$

Step 8

Calculate the coefficient rho from the following formula, using the results of Step 6 and Step 7:

$$rho = 1 - \frac{(\Sigma d^2 \times 6)}{N(N^2 - 1)}$$

Step 8

$$rho = 1 - \frac{(2 \times 6)}{6(6 \times 6 - 1)}$$

$$rho = 1 - \frac{12}{216 - 6}$$

$$rho = 1 - 0.0571429$$

$$rho = + 0.943$$

Step 9

Look up Table ST2.

Step 9

From Table ST2 we see this achieves a significance of $p \leqslant 0.01$ for a one-tailed test. We can conclude with some confidence that marriage partners choose someone with a similar level of attractiveness.

Table ST2 Spearman's rank-order correlation coefficient

N	Significance level		
	0.05	0.01	one-tailed list
	0.10	0.02	two-tailed list
4	1.000		
5	0.900	1.000	
6	0.829	0.943	
7	0.714	0.893	
8	0.643	0.833	
9	0.600	0.783	
10	0.564	0.746	
12	0.504	0.678	
14	0.464	0.626	
16	0.429	0.582	
18	0.401	0.550	
20	0.381	0.522	
22	0.361	0.498	
24	0.344	0.476	
26	0.330	0.457	
28	0.317	0.440	
30	0.306	0.425	

For numbers of pairs greater than N = 30 the critical value of the correlation coefficient alters only slightly, so this table is still appropriate.

(Adapted from Table P, S. Siegel, *Nonparametric Statistics for the Behavioural Sciences*, McGraw-Hill 1956.)

Using this table
Read across from *N* (the number of paired scores). Look for a value on the table that is **equal to or less than** the value of Spearman's rho. Look above that figure, to the top of the table, to see the level of significance achieved. Values for a two-tailed test are given below values for a one-tailed test. Note that values for a *two-tailed test* in the first column are *not* statistically significant.

Calculating Pearson's product moment coefficient

When to use the test

Additional requirements

Types of data   *Interval or ratio data.*

Other requirements   *Data must be parametric (fitting the normal curve of distribution and each sample having similar variance).*
Scattergram should show data do not curve.

What happens in the test
The paired data are compared using the *scores*. The test shows how closely each pair of scores are related to one another. The correlation coefficient formula makes use of the difference of the scores from the mean for each sample. This is why the data must be parametric to be used in this test.

A psychologist has developed a test for verbal reasoning. She tries it out on a pilot group of ten students. To see if the test is reliable she retests the students after two weeks, on the same test. She plots her data on two histograms and establishes that they tend towards the normal curve of distribution. She calculates the variance of her two samples and finds that they are quite similar. A scattergram demonstrates that the data do not curve.

The data are as follows

Participants	Test 1	Test 2
P1	26	29
P2	22	20
P3	43	39
P4	34	36
P4	15	15
P6	30	28
P7	11	9
P8	26	22
P9	27	25
P10	23	25

Cases	Score A	Score B	A^2	B^2	AB
P1					
P2					
P3					
etc.					
$N =$			$\sum A^2 =$	$\sum B^2 =$	$\sum AB =$

Step 1

Draw up a table for your data. See table above.

N is the total number of cases (pairs of scores).

Score A is the first variable in the pair; Score B is the second variable.

A^2 is the square of the scores of the first variable.

B^2 is the square of the scores of the second variable.

AB is the product of the scores of each variable.

Step 2

Fill in the paired data for each case putting the data for the first variable under Score A and data for the second variable under Score B.

Step 3

Square the data for your first variable and put in column A^2. Repeat for second variable.

Step 4

Multiply score A by score B for each case, and put in column AB.

Step 5

Calculate N and record, then add up the columns for A^2, B^2 and AB to obtain $\sum A^2$, $\sum B^2$ and $\sum AB$. (Remember that $\sum$ means 'sum of'.)

Steps 1–5

Draw up a table and fill in, as shown below.

Cases	Score A	Score B	A^2	B^2	AB
P1	26	29	676	841	754
P2	22	20	484	400	440
P3	43	39	1849	1521	1677
P4	34	36	1156	1296	1224
P5	15	15	225	225	225
P6	30	28	900	784	840
P7	11	9	121	81	99
P8	26	22	676	484	572
P9	27	25	729	625	675
P10	23	25	529	625	575
$N = 10$	$\sum A = 257$	$\sum B = 248$	$\sum A^2 = 7345$	$\sum B^2 = 6882$	$\sum AB = 7081$

111

Step 6

Calculate the following from the data in your table:

$\Rightarrow \quad N \times \Sigma AB$

$\Rightarrow \quad \Sigma A \times \Sigma B$

then find the value of

$\Rightarrow \quad (N \times \Sigma AB) - (\Sigma A \times \Sigma B)$

Step 6

	calculation	outcom
$N \times \Sigma AB$	10×7081	70810
$\Sigma A \times \Sigma B$	257×248	63736
$(N \times \Sigma AB) - (\Sigma A \times \Sigma B)$	70810–63736	7074

Step 7

Calculate the following:

$\Rightarrow \quad N \times \Sigma A^2$

$\Rightarrow \quad (\Sigma A)^2$

then find the value of

$\Rightarrow \quad (N \times \Sigma A^2) - (\Sigma A)^2$

Step 7

	calculation	outcom
$N \times \Sigma A^2$	10×7345	73450
$(\Sigma A)^2$	257×257	66049
$(N \times \Sigma A^2) - (\Sigma A)^2$	73450–66049	7401

Step 8

Calculate the following:

$\Rightarrow \quad N \times \Sigma B^2$

$\Rightarrow \quad (\Sigma B)^2$

then find the value of

$\Rightarrow \quad (N \times \Sigma B^2) - (\Sigma B)^2$

Step 8

	calculation	outcom
$N \times \Sigma B^2$	10×6882	68820
$(\Sigma B)^2$	248×248	61504
$(N \times \Sigma B^2) - (\Sigma B)^2$	68820–61504	7316

Step 9

Multiply the result of Step 7 and Step 8.

Step 9

7401×7316

$= 54145716$

Step 10

Calculate the square root of Step 9.

Step 10

$\sqrt{54145716}$

$= 7358.3773$

Step 11

Divide the result of Step 6 by the result of Step 10. This is the correlation coefficient *r*.

Step 11

$r = \dfrac{7074}{7358.3773}$

$r = 0.9614$

Step 12

Calculate the degrees of freedom. ($df = N - 2$) Look up the correlation coefficient on Table ST3. Find the row equivalent to the degrees of freedom and look up the significance level.

Step 12

$df = N - 2$
$df = 8$

Looking at ST3, with 8 degrees of freedom, for a one-tailed test, a correlation coefficient of 0.961 is significant at $p < 0.0005$
We can conclude that the test devised by the psychologist is very reliable. The results are highly consistent.

Table ST3 Pearson's *r* correlation coefficient

N− 2	Significance level			
	0.025	0.005	0.0005	one-tailed list
	0.05	0.01	0.001	two-tailed list
1	0.99692	0.999877	0.9999988	
2	0.95000	0.990000	0.99900	
3	0.8783	0.95873	0.99116	
4	0.8114	0.91720	0.97406	
5	0.7545	0.8745	0.95074	
6	0.7067	0.8343	0.92493	
7	0.6664	0.7977	0.8982	
8	0.6319	0.7646	0.8721	
9	0.6021	0.7348	0.8471	
10	0.5760	0.7079	0.8233	
11	0.5529	0.6835	0.8010	
12	0.5324	0.6614	0.7800	
13	0.5139	0.6411	0.7603	
14	0.4973	0.6226	0.7420	
15	0.4821	0.6055	0.7246	
16	0.4683	0.5897	0.7084	
17	0.4555	0.5751	0.6932	
18	0.4438	0.5614	0.6787	
19	0.4329	0.5487	0.6652	
20	0.4227	0.5368	0.6524	
25	0.3809	0.4860	0.6074	
30	0.3494	0.4487	0.5541	
35	0.3246	0.4182	0.5189	
40	0.3044	0.3932	0.4806	
45	0.2875	0.3721	0.4648	
50	0.2732	0.3541	0.4433	
60	0.2500	0.3248	0.4073	
70	0.2310	0.3017	0.3799	
80	0.2172	0.2830	0.3568	
90	0.2050	0.2673	0.3375	
100	0.1946	0.2540	0.3211	

(Adapted from Table VII, R. A. Fisher and F. Yates, *Statistical Tables for Biological, Agricultural and Medical Research*, 6th edn, Oliver & Boyd 1963.)

Using this table

Read across from *N−*2 (the number of paired scores *less* 2). Look for a value on the table that is **equal to or less than** the value of Pearson's *r*. Look above that figure, to the top of the table, to see the level of significance achieved. Values for a two-tailed test are given below values for a one-tailed test.

Tests of difference

The rest of the tests we will consider deal with differences between samples. If samples are statistically comparable, the more the scores in the samples differ, the more we can be confident that the IV has had an effect on the DV.

Tests where data are paired

When a design is repeated measures or matched groups, then the data collected are in *pairs*. We will consider three tests where such conditions apply. These are:

- The sign test
- Wilcoxon signed-rank test
- Related t-test

The first two are described as *non-parametric*. They deal with samples of data that are ordinal or where the data can be described as 'distribution free' (see Sandy MacRae *Drawing Inferences from Statistical Data* BPS Open Learning Units 1994). In other words, they can be used with data that does not meet strict criteria concerning the normal curve of distribution and also variance. The third test does require data that are 'distribution dependent'. It must be parametric, with data at the interval level of measurement, fitting the normal curve of distribution and of similar variance.

The sign test

When to use the test

Type of test	*Test of difference.*
Type of design	*Repeated measures or matched groups.*
Type of data	*Data are nominal (although raw data may be at least ordinal).*
Other requirements	*Data must be paired.*

What happens in the test
The sign test is probably the simplest statistical test. It shows the differences between pairs of scores. Even if the data you use are ordinal or interval, the sign test ignores their value and just takes account of whether one of a pair of scores is bigger than another. When we looked at the concept of probability on page 79, we considered an experiment looking at the effect of music on scores for a problem-solving test. We investigated the likelihood that one group of scores would be greater than the other. We ignored the *size* of the difference between each pair of scores and only noted when one was greater than the other. The sign test provides us with a simple and quick 'eyeball test' to show us if paired data are

significantly different. Below we will consider the results of research where a psychologist used a simple rating scale to compare paintings from two different traditions.

Calculation of the sign test

Calculations

Step 1

Draw up a table with data in pairs. For a repeated measures design the table would look like this:

Participants	Score A	Score B	Sign
P1			
P2			
P3			
P4			
etc.			

Enter the data for the pairs of scores.

Step 2

If the score for A is greater than B for any pair, put a '+' in the Score column; if A is smaller, put a '−'. For tied scores put a 0.

Examples

Steps 1–2

Draw up a table and fill in the relevant data, noting in the sign column where A is greater than (+), less than (−) or the same as (0) B. We will illustrate with ratings out of 7, given by 11 participants, to a traditional picture (A) and a modern abstract painting (B). A rating of 1 was low and 7 was high. The researcher did not predict which would be preferred, so the hypothesis has no direction (i.e., is two-tailed).

Table of ratings for two contrasting pictures

Participants	Score A	Score B	Sign
P1	6	3	+
P2	3	4	−
P3	5	2	+
P4	7	1	+
P5	3	6	−
P6	5	2	+
P7	7	4	+
P8	5	5	0
P9	2	3	−
P10	6	2	+
P11	5	1	+

Step 3

Count the number of positive and negative signs (ignoring any 0s). This is N.

Step 3

There are 7 '+' signs and 3 '−' signs. The tied score (P8) can be ignored.

$N = 10$.

Step 4

Count the number of the sign that occurs less frequently. This is your test statistic (S).

Step 5

Look it up on Table ST4, using N to show where you look at the table.

Step 4

The sign that occurs least is the minus. The test statistic is therefore 3.

$S = 3$

Step 5

On Table ST4 with a value for N of 10, the test statistic 3 is greater than the table value 1. The result is *not* significant at the 5% level.

Table ST4 Critical values of the sign test

N	0.05	0.025	0.01	one-tailed test
	0.10	0.05	0.02	two-tailed test
5	0	n/a	n/a	
6	0	0	n/a	
7	0	0	0	
8	1	0	0	
9	1	1	0	
10	1	1	0	
11	2	1	1	
12	2	2	1	
13	3	2	1	
14	3	2	2	
15	3	3	2	
16	4	3	2	
17	4	4	3	
18	5	4	3	
19	5	4	4	
20	5	5	4	
25	7	7	6	
30	10	9	8	
35	12	11	10	

Using this table
Read across from N (the number of paired scores). Look for a value on the table that is **equal to or greater than** the value of S. Look above

that figure, to the top of the table, to see the level of significance achieved. Values for a two-tailed test are given below values for a one-tailed test. Do note, values for a *two-tailed test* in the first column, are *not* statistically significant.

Adapted from F. Clegg, *Simple Statistics*, Cambridge University Press, 1982. With kind permission of the author and the publishers.

The Wilcoxon signed ranks test

When to use the test

Type of test   *Test of difference.*
Type of design   *Repeated measures or matched groups.*
Type of data   *Data are ordinal (or interval).*
Other requirements   *Data must be paired.*

What happens in the test
This test makes use of the size of the difference between scores. These differences are ranked (because the data cannot be considered as precise as interval data, and only the ranks are meaningful). The test shows significant *difference*. If all of the scores in one sample were bigger than their pairs in the other sample, a significant result would appear very likely. The Wilcoxon test looks at the ranks that go in the opposing direction to the majority. The smaller the total of these ranks, the greater the chance of a significant result.

Calculation of the Wilcoxon test

Calculations

Step 1

Draw up a table for the paired scores. (For a matched group design the table would need to be adapted with an extra Participant's column between Score A and Score B.)

Participants	Score A	Score B	Diff. d	Rank d
P1				
P2				
P3				
P4				
etc.				

Example

Step 1

To illustrate, we will use the same data that we used in the sign test. The scores represent ratings given by participants for two contrasting pictures. Using a scale of 1 to 7 they rated a traditional picture (A) and a modern abstract painting (B). 1 was low and 7 was high. The researcher did not predict which would be preferred, so the hypothesis has no direction (i.e., is two-tailed).

Step 2

Subtract Score *B* from Score *A* and put result in Difference (*d*) column. Put a '+' before a positive score, a '−' before a negative score and for tied scores put a '0'.

Step 2

Subtracting in the same direction for all the scores (*A* − *B*) gives the following result:

Score *A*	Score *B*	Diff. *d*
6	3	+3
3	4	−1
5	2	+3
7	1	+6
3	6	−3
5	2	+3
7	4	+3
5	5	0
2	3	−1
6	2	+4
5	1	+4

Step 3

Rank all the scores by size. Ignore the positive and negative signs for this process. Leave out the 0s (tied scores). For guidance on ranking scores see page 103.

Step 3

Put scores in size order, ignoring the signs. Ranks are shown in the shaded area in the table.

1	1	3	3	3	3	3	4	4	6
1	2	3	4	5	6	7	8	9	10
1.5	1.5	5	5	5	5	5	8.5	8.5	10

Put results in table as shown below; noting the signs.

Participants	Score A	Score B	Diff. d	Rank d
P1	6	3	+3	5
P2	3	4	−1	1.5
P3	5	2	+3	5
P4	7	1	+6	10
P5	3	6	−3	5
P6	5	2	+3	5
P7	7	4	+3	5
P8	5	5	0	
P9	2	3	−1	1.5
P10	6	2	+4	8.5
P11	5	1	+4	8.5

Step 4

Find the value of N by adding all the pairs of scores where there was a difference (i.e., ignoring any 0's).

Step 4

To find N add up all the pairs of scores where A is different from B (i.e., ignoring participant 8, with a tied score). $N = 10$.

Step 5

Add up the sum of all the positive scores. Separately add up the sum of all the negative scores. The smaller figure in this step is the test statistic T.

Step 5

Adding the ranks of the positive signs gives:
$5 + 5 + 10 + 5 + 5 + 8.5 + 8.5 = 47$

Adding the ranks of the negative signs gives:
$1.5 + 5 + 1.5 = 8$

$T = 8$

Step 6

Look up the result on Table ST5. Read across the table from the value of N. Test statistic T must be equal to or greater than the table value.

Step 6

Look up Table ST5. Reading across from $N = 10$ shows that 8 is equal to the table value for the 5% level for a two-tailed test. We can conclude that the experimental hypothesis can be accepted at a significance level of $p < 0.05$.
You will see that the result is **significant** for the Wilcoxon test, when the same data were not significant for the less sensitive sign test.

Table ST5 Critical values of the Wilcoxon test

N	0.05	0.025	0.01	one-tailed test
	0.10	0.05	0.02	two-tailed test
6	2	0	n/a	
7	3	2	0	
8	5	3	1	
9	8	5	3	
10	10	8	5	
11	13	10	7	
12	17	13	9	
13	21	17	12	
14	25	21	15	
15	30	25	19	
16	35	29	23	
17	41	34	27	
18	47	40	32	
19	53	46	37	
20	60	52	43	
21	67	58	49	
22	75	65	55	
23	83	73	62	
24	91	81	69	
25	100	89	76	

Using this table
Read across from N (the number of paired scores). Look for a value
on the table that is **equal to** or **greater than** the value of T. Look above
that figure, to the top of the table, to see the level of significance
achieved. Values for a two-tailed test are given below values for a one -
tailed test. Do note, values for a *two-tailed test* in the first column are
not statistically significant.

Adapted from A. Edwards and R. Talbot, *The Hard-Pressed Researcher*
Longman 1994. With kind permission of the author and the publishers.

The related t-test

When to use the test

Type of test   *Test of difference.*

Type of design   *Related design; can be matched groups; scores in pairs.*

Type of data   *Interval.*

Other requirements   *Data is distribution dependent; in other words it must accord to the normal curve of distribution and both samples need a similar variance.*

What happens in the test

The t-test is a powerful way of investigating whether there are differences between two samples of data. In the computation, the data for both samples are compared to see the probability that they have come from *different* distributions. The simplest formula uses the standard deviation. If your calculator has the *sd* function for *populations* then the following formula will work:

$$t = \frac{\text{mean } d}{\sqrt{(sd)^2/N}}$$

- where *d* is the differences between the sample scores
- $(sd)^2$ is the variance of *d* (the standard deviation for the population, squared)
- *N* is the number of paired samples.

The method given below uses a different formula and assumes you do not have an easy way of calculating the standard deviation of the differences between the scores.

A psychologist investigates the 'Stroop Effect'. He times 10 participants naming the colours on a list of 20 words that are printed in different colours. He also times the same participants naming the colours on a list of words, where the words are colours (e.g., 'red', 'green'). He controls for order effect and ensures none of his subjects are colour blind. The results he obtains are shown in the table below. His measurements are in seconds.

Calculation of the related t-test

Calculations	**Example**

Step 1

Draw up a table for your data.

Steps 1–8

Fill in a table as shown below.

Participants	Score A	Score B	Diff. d	d^2
P1				
P2				
P3				
P4				
etc.				
$N =$	Mean =	Mean =	Σd =	Σd^2 =

Step 2

Calculate the means for each set of scores.

Step 3

Subtract the scores with the lowest mean from the scores with the highest mean (e.g., if *B* has a higher mean, subtract *A* from *B*). Put result in column Diff. *d*.

Step 4

Square the outcome of Step 3 and put in column d^2.

Step 5

Add up all the figures in column Diff. *d* to get Σd.

Step 6

Add up all the figures in column d^2 to get Σd^2.

Step 7

Square the result of Step 5 to get $(\Sigma d)^2$.

Step 8

Find *N*, where *N* equals the number of paired scores.

Particip-ants	Score A in secs	Score B in secs	Diff. d	d^2
P1	13.3	9.3	4.0	16.0
P2	15.6	14.4	1.2	1.44
P3	18.2	16.2	2.0	4.0
P4	15.7	15.7	0.0	0.0
P5	15.6	13.5	2.1	4.41
P6	17.5	13.9	3.6	12.96
P7	14.7	14	0.7	0.49
P8	19.8	12.8	7.0	49.0
P9	18.2	15	3.2	10.24
P10	16.5	11.3	5.2	27.04
$N = 10$	Mean = 16.5	Mean = 13.61	Σd = 29	Σd^2 = 125.58

Step 9

Apply your results in this formula: (refer to Step 8, Step 5, Step 6 and Step 7)

$$\frac{(N \times \Sigma d^2) - (\Sigma d)^2}{N - 1}$$

Step 9

Apply the formula:

$$\frac{(10 \times 125.58) - (29 \times 29)}{10 - 1}$$

$$= \frac{1255.8 - 841}{9}$$

$$= 46.08888$$

Step 10

Find the square root of the result of Step 9.

Step 10

The square root of Step 9 is

$$\sqrt{46.08888}$$

$$= 6.7888798$$

Step 11

Divide Σd (the outcome of Step 5) by the outcome of step 10. This gives the test statistic t.

Step 11

$$\frac{29}{6.7888798}$$

$$t = 4.27169$$

Step 12

Calculate the degrees of freedom (df) $N - 1$; where N is the number of paired scores.

Step 12

$df = 10 - 1$
$\quad = 9$

Step 13

Look at Table ST6. Find the df value on the left-hand column. Read across from this degree of freedom, to a table value that is equal to or *less* than the value for t. Look up from this value to the level of significance.

Step 13

From Table ST6 we can see that our result for t is greater than the table value 3.25 at $df = 9$. This means that $p \leq 0.005$ for a one-tailed test. The result is highly significant.

Table ST6 Critical values of the t-test

Degrees of freedom	Significance level of 0.05 (one-tailed)	Significance level of 0.05 (two-tailed)	Significance level of 0.01 (one-tailed)	Significance level of 0.01 (two-tailed)
1	6.31	12.71	31.82	63.66
2	2.92	4.30	6.97	9.93
3	2.35	3.18	4.54	5.84
4	2.13	2.78	3.75	4.60
5	2.02	2.57	3.37	4.03
6	1.94	2.45	3.14	3.71
7	1.90	2.37	3.00	3.50
8	1.86	2.31	2.90	3.36
9	1.83	2.26	2.82	3.25
10	1.81	2.23	2.76	3.17
11	1.80	2.20	2.72	3.11
12	1.78	2.18	2.68	3.06
13	1.77	2.16	2.65	3.01
14	1.76	2.15	2.62	2.98
15	1.75	2.13	2.60	2.95
16	1.75	2.12	2.58	2.92
17	1.74	2.11	2.57	2.90
18	1.73	2.10	2.55	2.88
19	1.73	2.09	2.54	2.86
20	1.73	2.09	2.53	2.85
21	1.72	2.08	2.52	2.83
22	1.72	2.07	2.51	2.82
23	1.71	2.07	2.50	2.81
24	1.71	2.06	2.49	2.80
25	1.70	2.06	2.49	2.79
26	1.71	2.06	2.48	2.78
27	1.70	2.05	2.47	2.77
28	1.70	2.05	2.47	2.76
29	1.70	2.05	2.46	2.76
30	1.70	2.04	2.46	2.75
40	1.68	2.02	2.42	2.70
60	1.67	2.00	2.39	2.66
120	1.66	1.98	2.36	2.62
∞	1.65	1.96	2.33	2.58

(Adapted from Table III, R. A. Fisher and F. Yates, *Statistical Tables for Biological, Agricultural and Medical Research*, 6th edn, Oliver & Boyd 1963.)

Using this table

Read across from the relevant degree of freedom. Look for a value on the table that is **equal to or less than** the value of t. Look above that figure, to the top of the table, to see the level of significance achieved.

Tests where data are not paired

When a design is unrelated then the data that are collected are not in pairs. The experimental design will involve *two* groups. These will not necessarily be of the same size. There are two tests which we will look at, which fall into this category. These are:

● the Mann-Whitney U test

● the unrelated t-test.

The Mann-Whitney U test is described as *non-parametric*. Like some of the tests we have already considered, it is 'distribution free'. In other words the effective working of the test does not require that the data are normally distributed, nor that the distributions of each sample are of similar variance. With the unrelated t-test the data must be parametric, with data at the interval level of measurement fitting the normal curve and of similar variance.

The Mann-Whitney U test

When to use the test

Type of test   *Test of difference.*

Type of design   *Between groups; independent measures.*

Type of data   *Data must be ordinal (or interval).*

Other requirements   *The test as given here works for samples up to 20.*

> ### What happens in the test
> The test compares the *ranks* of each of the samples. As the data from both samples are ranked together, then the ranks for each sample are added up. The degree of *difference* between the sum of the ranks indicates the significance of the result. The more the sum of the ranks differ, the greater the significance.
>
> A student psychologist decides to test the hypothesis that perception is affected by hunger. She compared two groups, one made up of participants who had recently eaten, the other composed of participants who had not eaten anything in the previous three or more hours. All were shown a Crunchie Bar. They then individually had to estimate the size of the bar on a scale marked in centimetres. She predicts that the hungry participants will estimate the bar as longer than those who have recently eaten. The hypothesis is thus one-tailed. The results are shown in the table on page 127 as Score A and Score B on page 128.

Calculating the Mann-Whitney U test

<table>
<tr><th>**Calculations**</th><th>**Examples**</th></tr>
</table>

Calculations

Step 1

Draw up a table for the scores from each of the samples.

Group A	Score A	Rank A	Group B	Score B	Rank B
P1			P9		
P2			P10		
P3			P11		
P4			P12		
etc.			etc.		
N_a =		ΣR_a =	N_b =		ΣR_b =

Step 2

Put in the scores for each group, in participant order. Work out N_a and N_b. These are the number of participants in Group A and Group B.

Step 3

Write out *all* the scores for *both* groups in size order, and work out their ranks (see Ranking on page 103). Fill in the ranks for each score in columns Rank *A* and Rank *B*.

Examples

Step 1

For table see below.

Step 2

See table below.

Step 3

10.3	1	1		12.0	13	11.5
11.0	2	2.5		12.5	14	14
11.0	3	2.5		12.8	15	15
11.5	4	5.5		12.9	16	16
11.5	5	5.5		13.2	17	17
11.5	6	5.5		13.5	18	18
11.5	7	5.5		14.0	19	19.5
11.8	8	8.5		14.0	20	19.5
11.8	9	8.5		14.3	21	21
12.0	10	11.5		14.5	22	22
12.0	11	11.5		15.4	23	23
12.0	12	11.5				

Transfer results to table.

Step 4

Add up the ranks for each sample to obtain ΣR_a and ΣR_b.

Step 4

$\Sigma R_a = 186 \quad \Sigma R_b = 88$

Group A	Score A	Rank A	Group B	Score B	Rank B
P1	14.0	19.5	P14	11.5	5.5
P2	13.2	17.0	P15	11.0	2.5
P3	11.8	8.5	P16	11.8	8.5
P4	11.5	5.5	P17	11.0	2.5
P5	15.4	23.0	P18	12.9	16.0
P6	12.0	11.5	P19	12.0	11.5
P7	12.0	11.5	P20	14.5	22.0
P8	12.5	14.0	P21	10.3	1.0
P9	13.5	18.0	P22	12.8	15.0
P10	14.0	19.5	P23	11.5	5.5
P11	14.3	21.0			
P12	12.0	11.5			
P13	11.5	5.5			
$N_a = 13$		$\Sigma R_a = 186$	$N_b = 10$		$\Sigma R_b = 90$

Step 5

Multiply N_a and N_b.

Step 5

$N_a \times N_b = 130$

Step 6

Use the following formula to calculate U_a:

$$U_a = N_a \times N_b + \frac{N_a (N_a + 1)}{2} - \Sigma R_a$$

Step 6

$$U_a = 130 + \frac{13 (13 + 1)}{2} - 186$$

$U_a = 130 + 91 - 186$

$U_a = 35$

Step 7

Use the following formula to calculate U_b:

$$U_b = N_b \times N_b + \frac{N_b (N_b + 1)}{2} - \Sigma R_b$$

Step 7

$$U_b = 130 + \frac{10(10 + 1)}{2} - 90$$

$U_b = 130 + 55 - 90$

$U_b = 95$

Step 8

Take the smaller value from Steps 6 and 7 as your test statistic.

Step 8

The *smaller* value is U_a which is 35.

Step 9

Using N_a and N_b look up your test statistic on Table ST7. Read across from N_b and down from N_a.

Note

An alternative to Step 7 is to use:

$$U_b = N_a \times N_b - U_a$$

You can use the same formula to check your result as:

$$U_a + U_b = N_a \times N_b$$

Step 9

Table ST7 shows that the critical statistic for U is 33, when looking across from 10 (N_b) and down from 13(N_a). The calculated value is 35, which is higher than the critical value. The result is not significant at the 5% level for a two-tailed test.

Table ST7 Mann-Whitney U test

$$N_a$$

		4	5	6	7	8	9	10	11	12	13	14	15	16	17	18	19	20
	4	0	1	2	3	4	4	5	6	7	8	9	10	11	11	12	13	13
		–	–	0	0	1	1	2	2	3	3	4	5	5	6	6	7	8
	5	1	2	3	5	6	7	8	9	11	12	13	14	15	17	18	19	20
		–	0	1	1	2	3	4	5	6	7	7	8	9	10	11	12	13
	6	2	3	5	6	8	10	11	13	14	16	17	19	21	22	24	25	27
		0	1	2	3	4	5	6	7	9	10	11	12	13	15	16	17	18
	7	3	5	6	8	10	12	14	16	18	20	22	24	26	28	30	32	34
		0	1	3	4	6	7	9	10	12	13	15	16	18	19	21	22	24
	8	4	6	8	10	13	15	17	19	22	24	26	29	31	34	36	38	41
		1	2	4	6	7	9	11	13	15	17	18	20	22	24	26	28	30
	9	4	7	10	12	15	17	20	23	26	28	31	34	37	39	42	45	48
		1	3	5	7	9	11	13	16	18	20	22	24	27	29	31	33	36
	10	5	8	11	14	17	20	23	26	29	33	36	39	42	45	48	52	55
		2	4	6	9	11	13	16	18	21	24	26	29	31	34	37	39	42
	11	6	9	13	16	19	23	26	30	33	37	40	44	47	51	55	58	62
		2	5	7	10	13	16	18	21	24	27	30	33	36	39	42	45	48
N_b	**12**	7	11	14	18	22	26	29	33	37	41	45	49	53	57	61	65	69
		3	6	9	12	15	18	21	24	27	31	34	37	41	44	47	51	54
	13	8	12	16	20	24	28	33	37	41	45	50	54	59	63	67	72	76
		3	7	10	13	17	20	24	27	31	34	38	42	45	49	53	56	60
	14	9	13	17	22	26	31	36	40	45	50	55	59	64	67	74	78	83
		4	7	11	15	18	22	26	30	34	38	42	46	50	54	58	63	67
	15	10	14	19	24	29	34	39	44	49	54	59	64	70	75	80	85	90
		5	8	12	16	20	24	29	33	37	42	46	51	55	60	64	69	73
	16	11	15	21	26	31	37	42	47	53	59	64	70	75	81	86	92	98
		5	9	13	18	22	27	31	36	41	45	50	55	60	65	70	74	79
	17	11	17	22	28	34	39	45	51	57	63	67	75	81	87	93	99	105
		6	10	15	19	24	29	34	39	44	49	54	60	65	70	75	91	86
	18	12	18	24	30	36	42	48	55	61	67	74	80	86	93	99	106	112
		6	11	16	21	26	31	37	42	47	53	58	64	70	75	81	87	92
	19	13	19	25	32	38	45	52	58	65	72	78	85	92	99	106	113	119
		7	12	17	22	28	33	39	45	51	56	63	69	74	81	87	93	99
	20	13	20	27	34	41	48	55	62	69	76	83	90	98	105	112	119	127
		8	13	18	24	30	36	42	48	54	60	67	73	79	86	92	99	105

Using this table

N_a is the number in group A and N_b is the number in group B.
Upper figures represent a significance level of 0.05 for a two-tailed test (0.025 for a one-tailed test).
Lower figures (on the grey band) represent a significance level of 0.01 for a two-tailed test (0.005 for a one-tailed test).

The value for U (the smaller value of U obtained in your test), must be **equal to** or **lower than** the table value.

Adapted from A. Edwards and R. Talbot *The Hard-Pressed Researcher* Longman 1994. With kind permission of the authors and publishers.

The unrelated t-test

When to use the test

Type of test	*Test of difference.*
Type of design	*Between groups; independent measures.*
Type of data	*Interval.*
Other requirements	*Data are distribution dependent; in other words they must accord to the normal curve of distribution and both samples need a similar variance.*

What happens in the test

The test is establishing the degree of difference between the data in the two samples. Can they be considered as coming from *one* population of scores (in which case the null hypothesis will be accepted)? Or does it appear likely that they come from *two* populations of scores (supporting the experimental hypothesis)? If we were comparing the heights of basketball players and cricket players, we would expect their results to differ. We would want to know if our sample of basketball players appears to be significantly taller than the sample of cricketers. Does the basketball playing sample appear to come from an overall population that is significantly different from the cricketers?

To establish this, we use a statistic called the standard error (SE). The standard error is defined as the *standard deviation of the means of <u>samples</u>*. It is calculated from the mean and the standard deviation of any particular sample. (For those who really want to understand their statistics before using them, I recommend the discussion of this topic in Robson *Experimental Design and Statistics* or in MacRae *Drawing Inferences from Statistical Data*.)

The statistic *t* is then calculated using the following formula:

$$t = \frac{\text{Mean } A - \text{Mean } B}{SE}$$

This deceptively simple formula proves quite complex in practice. Taken step by step it is easy to follow. To illustrate, we will consider the case of a psychologist who wished to establish if caffeine aided reaction time. Controlling carefully for previous access to tea, coffee and other substances containing caffeine, she recruited *two* groups. One was made up of 15 people who had had some coffee or tea in the last three hours. They became her experimental group, and took an additional caffeine tablet. The other was made up of 17 people who had not taken any caffeine for three or more hours. They became her control group. She used a simple reaction test on a computer. The data collected are shown below. From these data she was able to discover if she can support a one-tailed hypothesis, that caffeine reduces reaction time.

Calculation of the unrelated t-test

Calculations

Step 1

Draw up a table for your data.

Group A	Score A	A^2	Group B	Score B	B^2
P1			P16		
P2			P17		
P3			P18		
P4			P19		
etc.			etc.		
$N_a =$			$N_b =$		
$\Sigma A =$			$\Sigma B =$		
		ΣA^2			ΣB^2
Mean $A =$			Mean $B =$		

Step 2

Add up the number of scores in each sample to find N_a and N_b.

Example

Step 1 to 5

Fill in the table as shown below.
Group A consists of the participants who took caffeine; Group B had not had any caffeine for the previous three hours.

Group A	Score A	A^2	Group B	Score B	B^2
P1	0.52	0.2704	P16	1.60	2.56
P2	1.22	1.4884	P17	1.31	1.7161
P3	0.81	0.6561	P18	0.96	0.9216
P4	1.11	1.2321	P19	0.97	0.9409
P5	1.20	1.44	P20	2.03	4.1209
P6	0.92	0.8464	P21	1.25	1.5625
P7	1.13	1.2769	P22	1.90	3.61
P8	1.54	2.3716	P23	1.59	2.5281
P9	0.67	0.4489	P24	1.56	2.4336
P10	0.57	0.3249	P25	1.38	1.9044
P11	1.06	1.1236	P26	0.71	0.5041
P12	0.99	0.9801	P27	1.77	3.1329
P13	1.10	1.21	P28	1.11	1.2321
P14	0.85	0.7225	P29	0.72	0.5184
P15	1.19	1.4161	P30	0.85	0.7225
			P31	1.19	1.4161
			P32	1.10	1.21
N_a = 15			N_b = 17		
$\Sigma A =$	14.88		$\Sigma B =$	22	
		ΣA^2 15.808			ΣB^2 31.0342
Mean $A = 0.992$			Mean $B = 1.294$		

Step 3

Calculate the means for each set of scores and record as ΣA and ΣB.

$$\bar{A} = \frac{\Sigma A}{N_a}$$

$$\bar{A} = \frac{\Sigma B}{N_b}$$

where Σ = 'sum of', $\bar{A}$ = mean for scores A and $\bar{B}$ = mean for scores B.

Step 4

Square the scores in each sample and put in column A^2 and column B^2.

Step 5

Add up the figures in columns A^2 and B^2 to get ΣA^2 and ΣB^2.

Step 6

Calculate $\Sigma A^2 - \dfrac{(\Sigma A)^2}{N_a}$

Step 6

$$15.808 - \frac{14.88 \times 14.88}{15}$$

$$= 15.808 - 14.76096$$

$$= 1.04704$$

Step 7

Calculate $\Sigma B^2 - \dfrac{(\Sigma B)^2}{N_b}$

Step 7

$$31.0342 - \frac{22 \times 22}{15}$$

$$= 31.0342 - 28.470588$$

$$= 2.56361176$$

Step 8

Add the result of Step 6 to the result of Step 7.

Step 8

$$1.04704 + 2.563611765$$

$$= 3.610651765$$

Step 9

Calculate $(N_a - 1) + (N_a - 1)$

Step 9

$$(15 - 1) + (17 - 1)$$

$$= 30$$

Step 10

Divide the result of Step 8 by the result of Step 9.

Step 10

$$\frac{3.610651765}{30}$$

$$= 0.120355059$$

Step 11

Calculate $\dfrac{1}{N_a} + \dfrac{1}{N_b}$

Step 11

$$\frac{1}{15} + \frac{1}{17}$$

$$= 0.0666666 + 0.0588235$$

$$= 0.1254902$$

Step 12

Multiply the result of Step 10 by the result of Step 11.

Step 12

$0.120355059 \times 0.1254902$

$$= 0.01510338$$

Step 13

To calculate the standard error (*SE*) find the square root of the result of Step 12.

Step 13

Standard error

$$SE = \sqrt{0.01510338}$$

$$= 0.12289581$$

Step 14

The test statistic *t* can now be found:

$$t = \frac{\bar{A} - \bar{B}}{SE}$$

Where $\bar{A}$ is mean of scores A, $\bar{B}$ is mean of scores B and *SE* is standard error for these scores. Whether the statistic is positive or negative does not matter.

Step 14

$$t = \frac{0.992 - 1.294}{0.12289581}$$

$$t = -2.45737$$

Step 15

Look at Table ST6 on page 125. The *df* value is $(N_a - 1) + (N_b - 1)$, as in Step 9. Find this value in the left-hand column. Read across from these degrees of freedom, to find a table value that is equal to or *less* than the statistic *t*. Look up from this value to find the level of significance.

Step 15

The *df* value is 30. Looking across from this point, we find that the table value of 2.46 is just smaller than our result for *t*. We can assume that, for a one-tailed test, we have established a significance of $p \leq 0.01$. Our psychologist has shown that caffeine appears to speed up reaction time.

The statistical tests – an overview

Test	Conditions	Comments
Chi² Test	• Test of association • Nominal data • Unrelated design • Data in cells must be independent • 2 × 2 requires an *expected frequency* of 5+	A significant association may *not* mean a causal connection
Spearman's rho	• Test of association • Correlational design • Repeated measures • Ordinal data • Paired scores that are related	Can cope with data that are slightly 'curved' A significant correlation may *not* mean a causal connection
Pearson's product moment	• Test of association • Correlational design • Repeated measures • Interval data • Data that are distribution dependent (parametric) • Paired scores that are related	Data must not be curved A more *powerful* test than Spearman's rho. A significant correlation may *not* mean a causal connection
Sign test	• Test of difference • Repeated measures or matched groups • Nominal data • Paired scores	Not a *powerful* test.
Wilcoxon signed ranks	• Test of difference • Repeated measures or matched groups • Ordinal data • Paired scores	Not as powerful as a t-test. Trustworthy with small samples where distribution (variance) can be difficult to judge; may avoid Type 1 error.
Related t-test	• Test of difference • Repeated measures or matched groups • Interval data Data are distribution dependent (parametric)	A powerful test. A robust test (especially with larger samples)
Mann-Whitney U test	• Test of difference • Independent measures • Ordinal data • (Tables in this book up to sample of 20)	Not as powerful as a t-test. Trustworthy with small samples where distribu-(variance) can be difficult to judge; may avoid Type 1 error.
Unrelated t-test	• Test of difference • Independent measures • Interval data • Data are distribution dependent (parametric)	A powerful test A robust test (especially with) larger samples)

Robust test	A test that can still produce a valid result, even if the necessary assumptions of the test are not met entirely.
Powerful tests	A test that is sensitive to small variations in data, when comparing samples. All tests become more powerful as the amout of data is increased.

Statistics questions

Statistics question 1

You carry out a survey of 24 male and female students to see whether there is a sex difference in the perceptual set. You record the number who see the old lady as compared to the young lady, in the famous ambiguous picture used by Leeper (1935).

a) What is the level of measurement of your data?

b) You carry out a Chi^2 test on your data. What is meant by the *expected frequency* in this test? What number must the expected frequency equal or exceed, in order for the test to be valid?

c) What are *degrees of freedom*? In this experiment, how many degrees of freedom are there?

d) What is Yates' Correction correcting for, in this test?

e) You find that your result is significant at $p \leqslant 0.05$ for a two-tailed test. Explain what this statement means.

f) This test is known as an inferential test. Explain the difference between inferential and descriptive statistics.

Statistics question 2

In an experiment you are interested in the degree of relationship between scores on a test of mathematical ability and a test of verbal reasoning skills. Both are scored out of 100 and have proved to be reliable tests.

	verbal reasoning	mathematical ability
P_1	40	35
P_2	85	67
P_3	71	73
P_4	79	87
P_5	65	63
P_6	45	49
P_7	58	52
P_8	66	69
P_9	92	93
$N = 9$		

a) Explain the term *order effect*. In conducting this study, how would you control for order effect?

b) Plot a scattergram for the scores. Does the scattergram indicate that a Pearson's Product Moment could be applied? Explain why/why not.

c) What other conditions would have to be met for a parametric test to be carried out?

d) A correlation of +0.91 was found on testing the results. This was significant for a one-tailed test at the 0.0005 level. What is the probability of making a Type I error in this experiment?

e) Define a Type II error.

f) To calculate the significance of a Pearson's Product Moment the value $N - 2$ is used. Another group of six students doing the same maths and verbal reasoning tests produced a correlation of +0.83. Using the simplified table below, state if this is significant, and to what level.

Level of significance for a:		
One-tailed test		
0.05	0.025	0.005
Two-tailed test		
$N - 2$ 0.1	0.05	0.01
3 0.80	0.87	0.95
4 0.72	0.81	0.91
5 0.66	0.75	0.87
6 0.62	0.70	0.83
7 0.58	0.66	0.79

(After Clegg)

Statistics question 3

You undertake a test of memory with two groups. They are randomly assigned and you have 12 in one group and 13 in the other. In one condition the words are arranged in categories (e.g., animals, trees, colours etc.). In the other, the words are presented in random order. You measure the number of words that are remembered after a one-minute gap.

a) What is the IV and the DV in this experiment?

b) Suggest a suitable Null Hypothesis.

c) Why is a Null Hypothesis used in an experiment?

d) What type of design is used in this experiment?

e) Define the following terms:
Interval Data
Ordinal Data

f) You discover your results are non-parametric. What statistical test would you use to see if your results are significant?

Statistics question 4

Below is a sketch of a Normal Curve of Distribution. The positions of one and two standard deviations on each side of the mean have been drawn. The mean score is 80 and the standard deviation is 10.

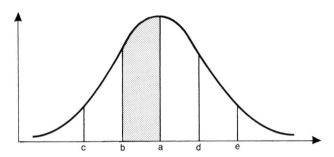

a) What percentage of scores fall in the shaded area between a and b?
b) Which line or lines represent the mean and the median?
c) What is meant by the term *standard deviation?*
d) What is the value or score represented at point e?
e) If 2.3% of the scores are above point e, what is the probability of achieving a score of e or above?

Statistics question 5

You are interested in the effects of prolonged television viewing on aggressive behaviour and attitudes of school children. You randomly select a sample of 100 students, using the school roll, at an 11–16 school. You carry out various tests, and administer a questionnaire and an attitude inventory.

a) What is your sampling frame?

b) What is your overall population?

c) Explain the value of having a random sample in this study. How might a random sample be selected from the school roll?

d) Explain what is meant by *demand characteristics.* How might demand characteristics influence the way pupils respond to the attitude inventory?

e) Suggest two ways in which you could assess the *reliability* of your attitude inventory.

f) Define validity, and explain why a reliable test may not always be valid.

Statistics question 6

You are studying preferences for soap operas on TV. Your ten subjects rate two popular programmes on a scale from 1 to 7, where the higher the score, the more the programme is liked. You are unsure which, if any, will prove more popular. The results are as follows:

	Neighbours	Eastenders
P_1	1	4
P_2	3	7
P_3	3	5
P_4	4	5
P_5	4	2
P_6	3	4
P_7	1	6
P_8	2	6
P_9	3	6
P_{10}	7	6

a) What type of design has been used in this experiment?

b) What level of measurement is achieved with these data?

c) Suggest an experimental hypothesis for this study. State if it is one- or two-tailed.

d) A Wilcoxon test is carried out, and Wilcoxon's T statistic = 7. This proves to be significant at the 0.05 level for a two-tailed test. Would it be more significant for a one-tailed test?

For guidance on how to answer these questions refer to pages 178–180.

Planning a practical

The careful planning of a practical can save a lot of heartache later. There are various stages in designing a practical.

1 Selecting a suitable problem to study.
2 Making sure that you have sufficient background material on the area you are interested in.
3 Deciding on a suitable design.
4 Developing the appropriate apparatus.
5 Clarifying the nature of the data you will collect and a suitable statistics test.

If each of these stages is carefully accomplished, then the practical can be successfully undertaken. Also, the writing of the report will not prove to be too burdensome. If you are following a course that requires a number of practicals to be completed, then it is as well to ensure that you choose ones with sufficient variety. This will ensure that you experience different techniques first hand and also that you practise a variety of statistical procedures.

We will now consider the steps in planning a practical in more detail. Students will find it helpful to write out brief responses to each of these steps *prior* to undertaking the practical. This will ensure that what they are going to do is feasible and can be accomplished.

Selecting a suitable problem to study

It is helpful, while you are following a course in Psychology, to keep one page at the back of your file for jotting down ideas that occur for practical work. Often something that you read, or an idea mentioned in a lecture or class discussion, can form the basis of a worthwhile investigation. If you are stuck, then thumbing through one or two good textbooks will provide a variety of ideas. You do not need to choose the exotic. A simple idea investigated appropriately and accurately is quite sufficient. Often it is quite acceptable just to replicate an idea that has been already tested. You may wish to add refinements or to develop your own ways of measuring the variables involved.

You need to ensure that there is sufficient background material on the topic that you are interested in to allow you to write your report. Particularly, when you are clear about what your independent variables are, you need to check that there is some background discussion that you can draw on which relates to those variables. For example, if gender is your independent variable in an experiment on memory, then you need to establish if there are any theoretical discussions or empirical studies that relate gender as such, to the specific aspect of memory you are considering. Judicious use of the indexes of text books, as well as careful searching of the library stacks, is important at this stage.

Developing a working hypothesis

During the planning stage you may not be able to formulate precisely the hypothesis that you wish to test. Nevertheless, at this stage it is most helpful to have a rough conjecture about what it is that you are investigating. When you have clarified what you are going to do, by reading and discussion, then you can formulate your hypotheses in a more scientific form. At this stage you need an idea to guide your planning.

Formulating the independent and dependent variables

It is vital that you are clear about what your variables are. Even for an observation or a correlation, you need to be clear on this point. In common parlance, you are deciding what is doing what to what. You are establishing what you think may be the causal links or associations in what you are investigating. Write them down. Then check that you have clearly specified what is manipulated in the independent variable and how change will be measured in the dependent variable. For a correlation or observation, be clear about how you will measure or record the changes or effects you are interested in.

Type of design and sample

Specify what type of design you are going to use. How many groups will you be investigating? Will the design be repeated measures, matched groups or independent measures? How will you choose your sample? How will they be allocated? If it is matched groups, what will be the criteria by which you will match your participants?

You need to decide on your sample size and their composition – in terms of age, class, sex, educational background and so on.

Controls

What controls will be necessary? Will you need to counterbalance to control for order effect? How will you ensure there is no experimenter effect – or operation of demand characteristics (where the participants do what they think you want them to do)? How will you control for extraneous variables? Where will you do your study and when?

Apparatus

This is where you *operationalise* your study. You need to design any apparatus that you are going to use. This will be particularly important if you are designing an attitude scale or a simple personality inventory. Even if you are using apparatus from some other source, you will need to check that it is appropriate to your needs.

Pilot study

In some instances, it will be advisable to carry out a brief pilot study to ensure that the apparatus you are going to use is appropriate, and that it works. In the light of this any necessary adjustments can be made.

Type of data expected

You should establish what sort of data your study will be likely to produce.

Type of statistical test to be used

In relation to the design you have chosen, and the data you expect to gather, you can decide what statistical tests are likely to be most appropriate. This will allow you to be sure that you do a spread of tests, and to avoid finding each experiment you do leads to the same statistical test.

Level of significance chosen

Another decision you need to make is about the level of significance that will be appropriate for your study. Generally a probability level of 0.05 will indicate that there is an effect taking place. If it is important to avoid a Type I error, however, then a lower level of probability should be chosen – say, 0.025 or 0.01.

References

Keep careful notes of the books you use. As you come across references you find useful, you will need to note where the studies come from. You will need the author, date of publication, the title, and publisher. For example:

Evans C. (1984) *Landscapes of the night: How and Why We Dream*, New York, Viking.

For further guidance on references, see page 2.

Ethical considerations

When you undertake a practical, you have an impact on others. You must consider whether the work you intend to do meets the ethical guidelines suggested by psychologists. You should be given guidance on this by your lecturer or tutor. The British Psychological Society and the Association for the Teaching of Psychology both provide written guidelines. These issues are also covered in many of the texts. Only some of the key points to consider are given here. They revolve around the question of your competence and knowledge, allowing the potential participants informed freedom of choice before they undertake to assist you, ensuring their safety and well-being, not infringing anyone's rights and ensuring true confidentiality.

Competence

Are you skilful enough to undertake the work that you propose? Is it an appropriate level of work? You should always check this with your lecturer before starting a study.

Well-being of the participants

This is the crux of the issue. You should do nothing that impairs the well-being of those who assist you. This means that, in approaching potential participants, they should be given sufficient information to make a proper choice about whether they would like to participate or not. If they agree, then the experiment itself should be undertaken in conditions of safety and in such a way that the dignity of the participants is sustained. They should have the right to withdraw if they wish. At the conclusion of their participation, they should be given as full a de-briefing as is appropriate. They should be thanked.

Work with children will involve all the above and obtaining clear consent from parents and/or teachers. Such research should always be fully discussed with someone competent, before you start.

Work with the elderly or those with special needs will similarly require special forethought.

The issue of consent does not arise in the same way with observation or natural experiments. However, the dignity of the individuals concerned should be respected and also the issue of confidentiality.

Confidentiality

In writing your report the confidentiality of your participants must be sustained. Generally you will refer to them as P1, P2, etc. If names are necessary, then use fictitious ones. Your own raw data and records should be kept carefully to ensure that confidentiality is not breached.

Other considerations

You should not make up data or copy the work of another. For most examination boards this will result in your disqualification. It is cheating.

Work with animals should be undertaken only after careful consultation with your psychology teacher. Animals should be subjected to a minimum of disturbance and not to any distress. Work with animals (strictly non-human animals) is not acceptable to some examination boards. You should check with your teacher or tutor.

Writing up the psychology practical

Having successfully completed a piece of practical work, it is then necessary to produce a report. This requires both a specific format and a certain style of writing. The approach is different from the style that you may use in essays. Also the order in which you write about things needs to be standardised. This will be dealt with below. With regard to the style, you will need to adopt an impersonal phraseology. Instead of saying 'I did such and such', you need to use phrases like 'the experimenter did ...'. Avoid saying 'we found that ...' and say rather 'the experiment showed that ...' or 'it was observed that ...'.

What follows is a checklist of points that you need to cover in a report. As the reports form part of the examination assessment, you need to ensure that you cover all the parts of all the sections in your writing or you run the risk of losing marks. Each heading below should form part of your account. However, some adjustments need to be made for observational studies.

Abstract

This is a *brief* summary of the *whole* report – 100 to 150 words maximum. It should touch on:

the problem being investigated

type of experimental method/design

subjects – who?
          – how many?
          – how selected?

IV and DV or variables in correlation/observation

experimental hypothesis (not word for word, but summarised)

main results – literally in a sentence
             – statistical test used, if any
             – significant or not at what level

Introduction

This introduces the area you are studying, and your particular experiment. It is mainly a *critical* summary of related studies. It should deal with:

relevant theory

relevant studies, with names/dates/basic findings

studies/theory relating to your *actual* IV/DV (e.g., if gender is a variable then gender must be dealt with to some extent in the introduction); if yours is a modification of an existing experiment give sufficient detail about this original experiment

make a link from the general introduction to what your experiment will focus upon

briefly introduce the key point/line/emphasis of your experiment

the aims of your experiment must be clarified here

brief details of pilot study could be given here (or in methods section, as appropriate), if one was undertaken

Method

The method section of the report consists of a number of subsections. Try to ensure that you do not repeat yourself in these sections. The procedure in particular should be kept to its own section and not allowed to spill over into the description of the design.

Design

State type of practical, i.e., observation or experiment; correlation or inferential etc.

State design, e.g., repeated measures, independent measures etc.

Very brief explanation as to *why* this design was chosen (no more than a sentence).

Variables (even in an observation and correlation)
   – IV
   – DV
Be precise; your definition of variables must be in terms of what actually varied (e.g., the *increase* in ...; the *score* attained ...)
   – Very brief reference to scoring/measurement used (e.g., score on personality test; number of dots made in one minute ...)

State experimental hypothesis
This should be constructed in terms of the IV and DV where appropriate. It should be one concise sentence.

State Null Hypothesis
This should also relate to the IV and DV but indicate that no *significant relationship* is expected.

Controls used should be outlined here – detail can appear in procedure, if necessary (e.g., mention that design was *counterbalanced*; mention age/sex controlled for, etc.).

Subjects

The number of subjects (and the population they represent, where appropriate)

Gender; age; class/educational background (as appropriate)

How selected

Apparatus

List all the materials, equipment used

Diagrams where necessary

If schedules/tests used, either reproduce here or in appendix

Procedure

This section should be a simple, very concise, step-by-step summary of what the experimenter(s) and subjects had to do. All specific instructions given should be reproduced in full.

Experimental conditions; time of day, noise levels etc.

Detail of controls as necessary

State instructions clearly, e.g., in speech marks

State how any unforeseen problems were coped with

Results

This is a *summary* of your data – **not** all the raw data. It should be presented in a clear format, which relates to the hypothesis that you are testing. Usually there should be both a table of results and a graph.

The table to have a proper title and labels

Usually give the totals/means

If there are a lot of raw data, then simplify and summarise as appropriate

Put full raw data in appendix

Any graphs drawn must be graphs! In other words the two axes should show some sort of variable/variation. *Do not plot raw data subject by subject.* Where it is illustrative, the subjects may be put in rank order for one of the variables and plotted against the other variable.

Graph should have clear title and labels

Graph can be line, histogram or scattergram

Use colour or neat shading where necessary, to show comparisons

Graphs must show *patterns* or *trends* – do not draw just to fill up space

You should provide a short explanation of any graphs or tables

At the end of your summary of results you may comment (one or two sentences at the most) on what the results appear to show. Then go on to the statistical test.

Explain *why* you chose this statistical test in relation to:

Test of association or difference

Type of data

Parametric or non-parametric

Give relevant details, for example:

The statistical value obtained from the test (calculated value)

The critical value needed to meet the level of significance

The level of significance obtained (or not) e. g., $p = 0.05$

A brief comment on the level of significance obtained 0.05 or 0.025 or 0.01 or higher

Either here, or in the design section, put the level of significance that you are taking as being significant for your hypothesis. This relates to the issue of Type I and Type II errors. Basically, you need to state whether a probability of 0.05 is sufficient to reject the Null Hypothesis, or whether 0.01 is needed.

With an observation or a practical that does not involve statistics, the results section should be used to present your findings in as imaginative and illustrative a way as possible. Use diagrams, quotations, pictures, descriptions or whatever is helpful, to summarise what your investigation revealed.

Give a very brief conclusion (one or two sentences).

Discussion

This section is important and should be written with great care. You must ensure that you cover all the following:

A statement of what your results showed (one or two sentences)

This statement will generally mention the statistical test, the calculated and critical values, and the significance level used/obtained. State whether the Null Hypothesis or the Experimental Hypothesis was rejected.

Then discuss any other features of your findings (trends, key results, aspects of graphs etc.)

Highlight any particularly notable results

How do your results relate to the general theory/experimental background outlined in your introduction? This *must* be fully discussed. Refer to relevant studies and show how your work extends, supports or contradicts

149

Critically review the methodological weaknesses of your experiment (apparatus, procedure, controls, sample etc.)

In relation to this, thoroughly consider the question of reliability and validity of your measures of your variables

Suggest reasonable modifications/extensions (not just 'a bigger sample would have produced a significant result')

Comment on the statistical procedures used – particularly the issue of the *power* of the test and its robustness. Round off with a very brief conclusion, restating the hypothesis that was supported – and *not* using the word 'proof' or its derivatives

Designing and writing up a practical – two examples

In this section we will consider two practical reports. In the first we will look in detail at how the practical can be developed from an initial idea to its final written form. Then further practical report will be presented, with a commentary.

A practical on feedback

As suggested earlier in the book (pages 141–145) there are various stages to planning a practical. The first is to choose a suitable problem to study. In the example presented here, the choice is to consider the concept of *reinforcement,* which is part of Learning Theory. More specifically, we choose to look at *feedback* as an aspect of reinforcement. Having settled on an idea, the next step is to decide on a working hypothesis, which will guide the research. This can be simply stated as 'feedback will aid the learning process of a simple task'. This working hypothesis will allow you to search the relevant text books to see if there is sufficient background material to provide a theoretical basis for an experiment in this area. Most general texts have considerable space devoted to the topic of reinforcement in general and some material on feedback as such. In addition, any specialist books on learning theory will have more detailed information.

Having scanned the texts, it becomes possible to choose the actual way in which the concept of feedback can be 'operationalised' into something that can be actually tested. There are many ways in which this could be done. One of the simplest is to set up a situation in which there is feedback against one in which there is not. The task could be anything that allowed reasonably accurate measurement; for example, inviting subjects to try to control the temperature of their fingertips. This could be measured with a sensitive thermometer. Even simpler is a task that involves drawing a line of a given length. The feedback would be in terms of by how far the line was drawn inaccurately.

Having chosen the task, a suitable design needs to be selected. The independent variable in this experiment will be whether feedback is given or not. The dependent variable will be the accuracy with which the line is drawn. It would be possible, with counterbalancing, to use a repeated measures design. However, an independent measures design using two groups will be used. This is chosen because a repetitive activity like drawing a line could prove boring if subjects had to do it too many times under the two different conditions.

A suitable size of sample also needs to be selected. Ten subjects under each condition should be sufficient to see if there is an effect.

The apparatus required will be sufficient sheets of blank paper, cut into squares of about three inches. A pencil, a ruler and a sheet to record results will be necessary, along with a sheet of standardised instructions. It will be helpful to carry out a brief pilot study to see if the method chosen actually works.

The data are going to be in terms of length. That is, the degree to which the lines drawn are inaccurate. The data therefore will be interval. If they prove to be parametric, then it will be possible to do an independent t-test (see page 131). If not, then a Mann-Whitney will be chosen. The level of significance selected for this experiment, will be $p \leq 0.05$ for a one-tailed test.

The effect of feedback on the accuracy of performing a manual skill

The title should be informative about the nature of the study without being overlong.

Abstract

This study tests the concept of feedback, in terms of information given to participants about a manual task they are to perform. 20 participants were chosen through an opportunity sample. They were all college students. Using an independent measures design the experimental group were given feedback over their accuracy of drawing a line, the control group were not. A Mann-Whitney test showed that the degree of error was significantly different in the two groups, at a significance level of $p \leq 0.05$, for a one-tailed test.

The abstract should be short and entirely to the point. The reader needs to know the purpose of the experiment, the design, and the basic results.

Introduction

When carrying out almost any activity animals and humans receive feedback. In this sense 'feedback' means information concerning the action undertaken. An airline pilot monitoring the dials of his controls and the schoolgirl receiving a mark for her French exam are both obtaining feedback. This information allows them to adjust their behaviour. As such the information can support what they are doing (positive reinforcement) or indicate a change is necessary (negative reinforcement).

Even if the term that is central to your study is quite well known, it is helpful to provide a brief definition, relevant to your study.

The concept of feedback is a central part of cybernetic theory, which considers how systems (animate and inanimate) can be self-controlling. In this theory a positive feedback will tend to continue or enhance an action or behaviour, a

Having defined terms in the first paragraph, this second paragraph begins to put the terms in context.

negative feedback will decrease or stop or reverse the original response. The homeostatic mechanisms of the body utilise feedback systems to keep aspects of the body's functioning, like temperature, at a constant level.

In learning a skill, the necessity of feedback becomes apparent. It is much easier to draw accurately with eyes open than with eyes closed, because of the visual feedback. If the skill is control over autonomic responses, then such feedback becomes essential. Studies of *biofeedback* have shown that autonomic responses can be controlled voluntarily. Miller and Dicara (1967) demonstrated this with rats. Their work with paralysed rats has been criticised and has proved difficult to replicate (Walker, 1984). However, this work stimulated much further research into biofeedback. There has been some success with reducing high blood pressure (Blanchard and Young, 1974).

Specific examples are important, but need not be dealt with at great length.

Give some names and dates to back up the points that you are making about studies. However, it is more important that you develop the concepts relevant to *your* study, than to provide a long list of studies.

The concept of feedback is important also in the field of training. Here it is called 'knowledge of results'. It has been classified by Holding (1965) as artificial or intrinsic, verbal or non-verbal, terminal or concurrent. Feedback which occurs during the training period can produce dramatic increases in accuracy (Annett, 1969). The more detailed the feedback that is given, the more accurate the response tends to be.

During training, feedback provides a monitoring function (Bartlett, 1947) and is the essence of a skill, as compared to a habit. When learning a skill, the type of feedback needed tends to be different from the phase of improving or mastering a skill. The early stages require a verbal feedback which enables verbal-motor control (Adams, 1971). Later, motor control takes over. The classic example is learning to drive. Initially, verbal directions from the instructor are vital. After the basics have been mastered, the feedback comes intrinsically from the bodily-muscular sensations involved in the various aspects of driving, and visual feedback, in terms of where the car is headed!

This work is of direct relevance to the actual study covered in this report. Your introduction should gradually focus in precisely on your aim and purpose.

Aim

The aim of this experiment is to look at the value of verbal feedback in a simple training situation. The task chosen is drawing freehand, as accurately as possible, a 10 cm line. The conditions are also simple, involving the presence or absence of verbal feedback. The expectation is that verbal feedback will produce greater accuracy, and a diminishment of error.

A brief statement of your aim is essential. This is different from the hypothesis, and rather provides the general background for the specific hypothesis.

Method

Design

The experiment used two groups. The design was independent measures, with the experimental group receiving feedback and the control group receiving no feedback.

The independent variable (IV) is whether the group received feedback or not.

The dependent variable (DV) is the degree of error, measured in millimetres, for drawing an 10 cm line.

The <u>experimental hypothesis</u> is that receiving feedback in terms of degree of error will significantly reduce the error as measured in millimetres, when drawing a line of a given length.

The <u>null hypothesis</u> is that feedback will have no significant effect on the degree of error, as measured in millimetres, when drawing a line of a given length.

The controls for the experiment were:
1 using standardised instructions
2 using identical apparatus for each participant
3 using participants of a similar age and educational background
4 random allocation of participants to the two groups
5 testing participants in a similar environment

Do state how many groups are involved in a design. Then give the type of design.

By clarifying the IV and then the DV, it makes the hypothesis, which is essentially the relationship between the two, easier to formulate.

Remember to state that in the null hypothesis there will be no *significant* difference, not that there will be no difference.

Subjects

Twenty participants were used. They were all college students. There were 12 females and 8 males. The participants were chosen as an opportunity sample. They were randomly allocated to the two groups by alternating the allocation of participants to each group as they were chosen. There were two experimenters.

It is helpful to state the number of experimenters involved in an experiment.

Apparatus

1 1200 pieces of paper about three inches square
2 one pencil and one pencil sharpener
3 one ruler
4 standardised verbal instructions
5 a record sheet

Procedure

1 A participant was chosen and asked to participate in the psychology experiment. If they agreed they came to a small room and sat at a table. They were allocated to the experimental group or the control as appropriate.

Where allocation to groups is more elaborate, then the procedure should be explained at this stage.

153

2 The participant read the following instructions:
'I would like you to draw a line ten centimetres long on the pieces of paper that I will give you. Please start your line at the cross that I draw on the paper. I will/will not give you feedback on how close your line is to ten centimetres.'

If instructions are long they can be put in the appendix.

3 The participant drew the line.
4 The paper was removed, the line measured and its length recorded on the record sheet.
5 Feedback was given to the experimental group in terms of the number of millimetres their line was short or long. No feedback was given to the control group.
6 The procedure was repeated ten times with each participant.
7 The purpose of the experiment was explained to the participant and then they were thanked for their participation.

Always de-brief your participants. This is more than just courtesy, it is the only ethical way of proceeding.

Results

Table showing mean error of participants, measured in millimetres.

Feedback group		Non-feedback group	
P1	9.0	P11	18.6
P2	7.3	P12	12.9
P3	5.4	P13	6.4
P4	6.7	P14	10.7
P5	10.9	P15	14.5
P6	2.7	P16	26.3
P7	10.1	P17	29.9
P8	3.7	P18	5.5
P9	8.2	P19	23.1
P10	9.4	P20	21.0
Total:	73.4		168.9
Mean:	7.34 mm		16.89 mm

Make sure all your tables have a suitable heading.

In this table the degree of error made by each participant is shown, calculated by adding the mean of all their errors together, but ignoring whether the error was of positive or negative value. It is clear that the non-feedback group had a considerably greater margin of error. (For raw data see appendix.)

Give sufficient explanation of a table to make its meaning clear. A brief, one-sentence comment may be appropriate.

A chart showing the mean error of each of the partici-pants, for each trial, taking account of the sign.

Be sure that your charts have an adequate heading, and that each axis is labelled.

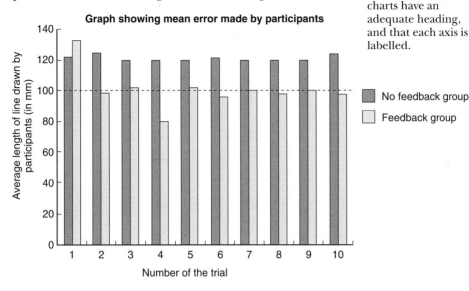

The points on this chart are made by adding the error for each participant at each trial, taking account of the sign (direction of error) and calculating the mean for each group.

The chart shows the effect of giving feedback. There is a clear tendency for the results of the experimental group to oscillate around the 100 mm line. The control group consis-tently overestimates the length of the line.

Again, a very brief comment may be of value, to indicate what the chart is illustrating.

Statistical test and level of significance

The level of significance chosen is $p \leqslant 0.05$. This is by con-vention. The data are of at least interval status. However, they are not normally distributed and so a Mann-Whitney test was carried out. This test is appropriate or an indepen-dent measures design on data of at least ordinal status.

The value of U was found to be = 15. This is significant for a one-tailed test at $p \leqslant 0.005$. The null hypothesis is therefore rejected and the experimental hypothesis supported.

If you choose another level of significance, say 0.01, you need to explain why (possibly in terms of avoiding a Type I error).

Be sure to specify one- or two-tailed, for the test.

Discussion

The results of the Mann-Whitney test indicated that feed-back is important in producing accuracy in a manual task. The experimental hypothesis was supported, and the proba-bility level achieved of 0.005 suggested strong support for the hypothesis. The other aspect of the study, that the effect of feedback would be cumulative, with a diminishment in error, was not framed specifically as an hypothesis. There is support for this provided by the graph. This indicates that

It is not obligatory, but it is helpful, to start by considering the actual results achieved.

the feedback group, which had an error in the first trial greater than the control group, achieved a greater accuracy by the second trial, which they were able to maintain. The results of the feedback group show that they tended to ossilate around the 10 cm line. The non-feedback group remained generally 2 cm away from the line. The raw data (given in the appendix) demonstrate the considerably greater erratic nature of the control group's results.

The findings, indicated by tables or graphs, should be briefly commented upon.

Although the results were significant, the test was not the most sensitive that could be used. The Mann-Whitney test is not as precise as the t-test. A higher level of significance might have been achieved with that test, had the results been fully parametric. A further analysis of the results to demonstrate the degree to which the experimental group learned over successive trials could also have been undertaken. The graph indicates that this is so, but a comparison of the degree of error in trials 2 to 5 with those in 6 to 10 would demonstrate if this was significant. A Wilcoxon test could have been used on the data from the experimental group alone.

Descriptive and inferential statistics both have room for error. The discussion should consider the likelihood of this error. Sometimes it can be that a test has not produced a significant result, but that it is clear that a more sensitive measure would be likely to do so. For example, a sign test may not be significant, where a Wilcoxon test is significant.

In general, the results of this experiment give support to the idea that feedback is necessary in training. Without knowledge of results (Holding), there is little possibility of the control group becoming more accurate. The only way they could become better would be if they do have an accurate notion of the length of a ten centimetre line, but need *practice* to learn to draw it accurately using freehand. This did not prove to be the case.

Make specific links back to studies or theories mentioned in the introduction.

The need for verbal-motor control, as suggested by Adams, during the early stages of learning a skill, is supported. Annett's suggestion that giving feedback concurrently with performance also appears to be supported, although it could be argued that the feedback was given at the end of each individual 'performance'.

You should be as rigorous as you can be in critically assessing what your results do, and do not, show.

The value of feedback does appear to be sustained in this study. However, some questions are raised. There is a confounding variable. Not only did the experimental group receive feedback, they also necessarily and at the same time received a verbal commentary on their work. The control group had only silence. This in itself could be considered a positive reinforcement, and consequently, the experimental group may have tried harder. The study could therefore have been measuring the effect of encouragement rather than the pure effect of information.

If you become aware of a weakness in your study then this is the place to explore it. You will not lose marks for spotting a flaw in an otherwise effective design.

This criticism could be met by a different way of conducting the experiment. Instead of the control group receiving no feedback, they could be told that their line was too big, or too small. This would be contrasted with the experimental

You need to comment on two aspects of your

group, who would be informed by how much their line was too big or too small. Both would be receiving feedback (and possibly positive reinforcement) but the experimental group would have more accurate feedback, enabling the hypothesis to be tested.

Another criticism of the experiment is the problem of boredom. Participants did appear to find the task a little tedious and perhaps did not concentrate. Although this was controlled for by keeping the task the same for both groups, a more interesting task could have been chosen.

A modification that could follow from this, would be to choose a task that is inherently more interesting. A computer game could be used, and played under two conditions, with sound on or with sound off. This would be appropriate, if the game led to a score that could be compared, and if the sound changed in a way that provided feedback to enable the game to be played more skilfully. Another possibility would be to take a manual and conceptual skill like solving a simple puzzle. The two conditions could involve different types of feedback which could be compared.

work. The first is the way in which your study could be modified to ensure that it measures what it is setting out to measure more effectively.

The second aspect is how your work could be extended. Here you will be looking not so much at improvements in technique as at ways in which the concepts could be elaborated or explored in more depth. The suggestions made should be feasible and appropriate for this level of work.

References

Legge D and Barber P *Information and Skill*, Methuen 1976
Cybernetics (pp 66–70) Holding; Annett; Adams
(pp 122–116)

Gross R *Psychology*, Edward Arnold, 1987
Biofeedback (pp 414–415)
Atkinson R, Atkinson R and Hilgard E *Introduction to Psychology* Harcourt Brace Jovanovich 1983
Biofeedback (pp 207–208)

Gleitman *Psychology*, Norton, 1981
Negative and positive feedback (pp 57–58)

See pages 2–6 for guidance.

Appendix

No appendix will be given here for reasons of space, but all the raw data and the workings of the Mann-Whitney test would be in the appendix.

A practical looking into the possible causes of social facilitation.

Abstract

The following practical is investigating social facilitation. This is how the presence of another person or group can affect our performance. In some instances performance can be facilitated, that is to say, enhanced, so that we either perform faster or more accurately or both. In other cases

'An investigation of …' rather than 'A practical looking into …' might be a better phrase for a title.

the performance can be impaired so that we perform more slowly or less accurately. There are several theories attempting to explain this process though this practical dealt with the evaluation apprehension theory. This was first proposed by Cotterall *et al.* (1968). This theory believes that social facilitation occurs because of our belief that we are being judged. Therefore our performance is slowed if it is new or complex, or enhanced if it is well learned or simple.

This first paragraph of the abstract is somewhat wordy. An abstract should be succinct – giving the bare bones of the whole investigation and its findings.

To investigate this theory, the practical used an adaptation of a Schmitt *et al.* (1986) experiment where participants had to perform either a simple task (in this experiment that will consist of crossing out upper-case letters in a passage) and a complex task (in this experiment that will involve performing maths questions). This was done to one of three conditions; alone, mere-presence and evaluation. This was also the same for this experiment where an independent design has been used to test a causal relationship. In total there were thirty participants who were selected by opportunity sample from lecture groups. The independent variable is whether or not participants are being evaluated or not. The dependent variable is the time it takes to perform the tasks.

This is a clear statement of what was investigated and why.

The experimental hypothesis states that participants will perform the simple task significantly faster in the evaluation condition but perform the complex task significantly more slowly in the evaluation condition. To support this, a significance level of 0.05 is being used by convention. Although the mean scores supported the experimental hypothesis, a Mann-Whitney test didn't produce a significant result for any of the data. Therefore the experimental hypothesis was rejected.

An appropriate synopsis of the results.

Introduction

This practical is investigating the possible cause of social facilitation. This has been described as the effect on an individual's behaviour by either a coactor (coactor effect), or an audience (audience effect). The effect on the individual is normally to improve the performance or task, in other words it 'facilitates' the performance. Although in western societies individual achievement is rewarded with high status, we must all at some point work either in a group – for example, as part of a management team. Or we have to perform in front of a group – for example, when presenting the findings of a report. The question is what causes our behaviour to be affected by the presence of the group or coactor. This will be discussed and investigated later; firstly, it is important to see how social facilitation was discovered.

One of the first experiments in social psychology was performed by Triplett (1898). This was set up on his observations of speed cyclists. Triplett noted that when a second cyclist or 'coactor' was present during the time trials the main cyclist would perform faster. In other words, the performance of the speed cyclist was facilitated by the presence of the second cyclist. Triplett set out to investigate this phenomenon in an experimental condition.

To do this Triplett used children as his participants; their task was to wind fishing reels as fast as they could for a set amount of time. The amount of winds was recorded and a second child or coactor was placed next to the participant and this time both had to wind the fishing reels. Triplett found that when the second person was present the amount of winds the participant performed went up; their performance was enhanced. Triplett termed this the coactor effect. Although the participants' performance in this experiment was enhanced, conflicting results have since been found.

Allport (1920) performed a series of experiments where participants had to perform either a simple task, such as crossing out all the vowels in a newspaper article, or a complex task such as multiplication questions. Allport found that with the simple task performance was facilitated by the presence of a coactor or audience. But with the complex task even though it was performed faster there were more mistakes made in the presence of others; the performance was therefore impaired.

The phenomenon of social facilitation is not exclusive to humans; Chen (1937) performed an experiment with working ants. In the first condition their rate of digging a certain depth whilst alone was recorded. In a second condition a second digger ant was placed next to the digger ant and again their rate of digging was recorded. Chen found that the working ant performed faster in the presence of the coactor. There have been several theories attempting to explain social facilitation; this practical is interested in the theory first proposed by Cottrell (1968). The other theories in this area will also be given an overview as this will be valuable in the evaluation of the experiment's findings.

One of the latest theories has been proposed by Baron (1986). In his theory Baron has used the fact that social facilitation occurs in animals as well as in humans to suggest that it is due to 'information overload'. According to Baron when we perform any task where there are other people present we have to pay some attention to the task and some to the audience or coactor. When the performance is simple or well learned it is easy to pay attention to both. This is because it is well within our limited processing capacity. But

These first four paragraphs are quite detailed. The writer is correct to put his work in a clear context, but a more concise summary of these early studies would be better.

if the task is complex or new we need to concentrate much harder on the task, therefore the effect that the presence of others has is to create 'information overload'.

Another theory proposed by Bond (1982), which is closely related to the theory this practical is interested in, is termed the self-presentation theory. Bond suggests that because we want to present a favourable image of ourselves, we are therefore concerned with our self-presentation. With a simple task or well-learned task this is possible because it is well within our capabilities, therefore we can perform it faster when others are watching. But a complex or new task is performed more slowly to avoid mistakes. This theory comes into question because social facilitation occurs in animals. An earlier experiment performed by Zajonc *et al.* also brings this theory into question because they demonstrate social facilitation in cockroaches. This experiment will be discussed later.

An earlier theory developed by Zajonc (1965) termed the 'drive theory of social facilitation' believed that the mere presence of a coactor or an audience led to an increase in arousal in both humans and animals and it is this that causes social facilitation. Zajonc claims that during times of heightened arousal individuals and animals are more likely to perform dominant responses. These can either be well-learned behaviours (such as playing a musical instrument) or instinctive behaviours (such as feeling aroused in stressful situations). According to Zajonc these dominant responses are either correct for that situation or incorrect. If they are correct then the performance is facilitated but if they are incorrect then the performance is impaired. The theory was demonstrated in a famous study using cockroaches.

> It is valuable to outline the various theories of social facilitation. This will provide references and concepts that can then be drawn on in the discussion at the end of the practical write-up.

In the experiment performed by Zajonc *et al.* (1968) cockroaches were placed into either a runway or a maze (below). The aim of this was that the cockroaches had to escape from a bright light. This was done by the cockroaches running into a darkened area.

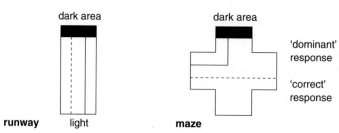

The results found that the cockroaches ran the runway faster in the presence of either a coactor or an audience (these were made up of other cockroaches). But they ran the maze slower when the coactor or audience was present. This, Zajonc *et al.* claim, is because in the runway the dominant response was the same as the 'correct response', therefore correct in that situation. But in the maze the dominant response was different from the 'correct response' therefore incorrect, thereby impairing the performance in the presence of other cockroaches. Hunt and Hillery (1973) performed a similar study to Zajonc *et al.* but used humans and arrived at the same conclusions. From this and other observations Zajonc argues that social facilitation occurs simply because of the presence of others.

> Again, the writer is a bit too detailed here.

The drive theory of social facilitation has been criticised by some who claim that there is more to social facilitation than simply the presence of others. They claim that it is also to do with the fact that there is always the feeling that behaviour is constantly being evaluated. Even in experiments where participants are left alone, they are aware that the results they produce will be evaluated (or compared against another participant's score) although facilitation will be reduced in experiments because the evaluation is normally performed in confidence. As stated earlier, it is this theory of evaluation that this practical is interested in.

> This is a crucial criticism, as it forms the basis of the writer's own study.

The theory of evaluation – appraisal was first proposed by Cottrell *et al.* (1968). They placed participants in front of an audience to give a presentation; there were two conditions to this experiment. In the first condition the audience was blindfolded (this allowed the participant to believe that they could not be evaluated, they were merely present), and in the second condition the audience could see the participant (therefore evaluate). The results showed that the competence of the performance dropped in the second condition and in the first condition the performance was facilitated. Cottrell *et al.* use this as evidence that it is the 'fear' of being evaluated that produces an impaired performance.

Further support for this theory was produced by Paulus and Murdock (1971). They also asked participants to perform in front of an audience in two conditions. Firstly they were told that the audience was composed of people who were of a higher status than the participant (therefore in a position to evaluate). In the second condition the participants were told that the audience was made up of fellow students (less likely to evaluate). They found that when the participants felt that their performance was being evaluated (as in the first condition) social facilitation dropped and the performance was impaired. But when the participants felt that their performance wasn't being evaluated their performance was facilitated.

To test the theory that social facilitation is due to individuals believing that their performance is being evaluated and not simply because of the mere presence of other people, this experiment will replicate Schmitt *et al.*'s 1986 study. In this study Schmitt *et al.* used three conditions whilst participants performed either a simple task (this involved the participant typing their name) or a complex task (getting the participant to type their name backwards and placing ascending numbers between each letter). The three conditions included the participant performing the tasks alone (control), with another person in the room but wearing headphones and a blindfold (the mere presence). Finally, with another person actually watching the performance (evaluation).

The work of Schmitt (1986) is left to the end. This is helpful, as the writer uses this as the basis of their own work. It means that the aim which follows develops logically from what is written here.

The results showed that when participants performed the simple task in the mere presence condition the task was facilitated (the control was performed in 15 seconds, the mere presence was performed in ten seconds). However, when the participants believed they were being evaluated the speed increased to seven seconds. In the complex task the performance in both the mere presence and evaluation conditions was slower than in the control condition (although the mere presence was slowest).

It seems then that when humans perform either simple or complex tasks the view that the task is being evaluated can have an effect on how that task is performed. This could have serious implications in 'real life' events, as was mentioned earlier although in the western world individual effort is important, but quite often we have to interact with either others or groups.

Aim

The aim of this study is to test the theory that social facilitation is caused by participants believing that they are being evaluated. To test this theory the experiment performed by Schmitt *et al.* will be adapted and used. This will be done by asking participants to perform a simple task (the simple task will comprise participants writing a standard name, the amount of time this takes will be recorded) and also a complex task (this will mean writing the name backwards with corresponding numbers e.g. A=1, again this will be timed).

This is a clear statement of aim. Overall, the introduction is very thorough but is rather on the long side. Detail could have been summarised in places, without losing clarity in terms of introducing concepts and mentioning studies.

Method

Design

This practical used an experimental type to test a causal relationship between the IV and the DV. The design was independent measures, this was to stop participants performing the tasks better because they had learned them or worse due to fatigue and not due to experimental reasons.

The description of the design is suitable. The justification of the design is effective.

Independent variable

The IV is whether participants are being evaluated or not.

Dependent variable

The time it takes participants to perform the simple task and the complex task. This will be done by timing participants on a stop-clock to see how long it takes them to perform the tasks.

Experimental hypothesis

Participants will perform the simple task significantly faster and the complex task significantly more slowly if participants believe they are being evaluated, compared to simply being in the mere presence of another person.

This is a one-tailed hypothesis, a significant level of $p \leq 0.05$ is being used to support the hypothesis. This is by convention.

The hypothesis is stated in a way that is testable and is clearly related to the theory in the introduction. It is important to say if it is one-tailed, what level of significance is chosen and why. This is an effective way to do it.

Null hypothesis

There will be no significant difference between the time it takes participants to perform the simple and complex task if they believe they are being evaluated compared to simply being in the mere presence of another person.

Controls

The tasks were counterbalanced.

How counterbalancing was achieved should be stated here (or in the procedure section).

Participants

In total there were thirty participants of whom twelve were male and eighteen were female. They were selected by opportunity sample from lecture groups around the college. To make sure at the end of the experiment that there had been the same number of participants performing each of the conditions, participants performed the conditions in the order 'alone', 'mere presence' and 'evaluation' condition (depending on what the last participant performed).

It is useful to state how many experimenters were involved. This is a good place to do so.

Apparatus

- Stop-clock with a 'green' button to start the clock and a red button to stop the clock.
- Paper/pen
- Standard paragraph: see appendix one
- Standard maths questions: see appendix one

Procedure

Once participants had agreed to take part in the experiment (on the understanding that they may stop at any time without any questions being asked) they were taken to the room. Because there were three conditions of which two required the participant to work on their own there were two briefings.

Alone and mere presence

The only difference between these two conditions was that in the mere-presence condition 'another' person was in the room (this person simply sat in the room with their back to the participant and read a book, they took no active role during the experiment). Participants were seated and told to read the bold type at the start of either passage (passage A, appendix one) or the top of the maths sheet (sheet A, appendix one), then;

> 'Do you understand the instructions at the top of the passage/sheet.' If they answered 'no' the instructions were verbally explained, then;

> 'Would you please carry out the task as quickly as possible, and start the clock once I have left the room. When you have finished please open the door to indicate this. Are you happy with what you have to do?' If they replied 'yes' the experimenter then left the room; if not the instructions were repeated.

Once the door was opened the experimenter re-entered the room. At the end of the first task they were told to wait a few moments whilst the next task was set up, the instructions (above) were repeated. If they had finished both tasks they were thanked for taking part in the practical and given a simple overview of the experiment and its aims. They were asked if they had any questions. If not, they were again thanked and left.

It is good to see that participants were properly debriefed and thanked.

Evaluation

The procedure was slightly different because participants were actually timed by the experimenter.

Once participants were seated they were told that they would be performing two tasks. They were then told to read the bold type at the top of either the passage (passage appendix one) or sheet (sheet B), depending on the t the participant was performing.

'Do you understand the instructions?' If they replied they were then told, 'The two tasks will be timed, start the first task when you are ready. When yo finished please indicate this by saying you have fir The time started once they picked the pen t stopped once they had indicated they had finisheu. When they had finished the first task they were told, 'Thank you for that, please give me a few moments to set up the next task.'

When this was done the procedure for the first task was repeated. Once both tasks had been completed they were thanked and given a brief overview of the experiment and then asked if they had any questions. If there were none they were again thanked and left.

Results
A full evaluation of what the results show will be given in the discussion section. A simple observation of the two tables (below) shows that participants on average performed the simple task (table two) faster when they perceived that they were being evaluated. This was predicted in the hypothesis. In the complex task (table one) participants' performances were slower when they perceived they were being evaluated and faster on their own. Again this was predicted. The full raw data are shown in appendix two.

A very short commentary on the results like this, just stating facts, is helpful.

Table one shows the descriptive results for the complex task.

	Alone (control)	**Mere presence**	**Evaluation**
Total	810	854	992
Mean	81.0	85.4	99.2
Median	67.5	87.0	93.5
SD	34.1	26.9	42.6
Range	119	98	124
Mistakes	1.5	2.1	1.8

The mistakes at the bottom of both tables indicates the average mistakes made by participants in each condition.

the descriptive results for the simple task.

	Alone (control)	Mere presence	Evaluation
	491	503	457
n	49.1	50.3	45.7
Median	49.5	46.5	45.0
SD	15.6	12.3	13.8
Range	49	45	38
Mistakes	1.4	2.1	1

Note that the tables are summaries, *not* raw data.

The difference can be seen more easily if the graph is looked at. From this it can be seen that in the simple task the difference is quite small. However, in the complex task there is a more marked difference in performance.

Table three below shows the results of the Spearman's rho on the data between the amount of mistakes made by participants and their time to perform the simple and complex task. It shows that only in the evaluation condition, whilst performing the complex task, was there a significant correlation between time and mistakes. In other words, the more slowly participants went the more mistakes they made.

This is the first of three statistical tests that the writer carried out. It is not usual to have to use a range of tests but it can be very useful on occasions.

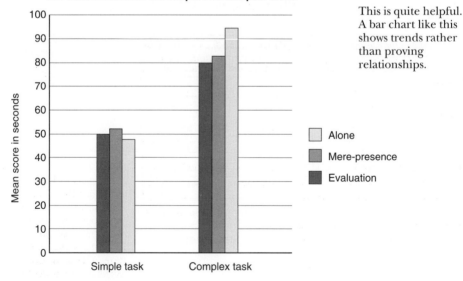

The mean results for the simple and complex tasks

This is quite helpful. A bar chart like this shows trends rather than proving relationships.

Table three shows the correlation between time taken to perform the simple and complex task and the amount of mistakes made.

	Simple	Complex
Alone condition	−0.1	−0.6
Mere-presence condition	0.1	0.1
Evaluation condition	−0.3	0.6

Significance test

The test used was the Mann-Whitney (U) test (although a t-test for unrelated data was used for participants performing the alone and mere-presence doing the complex task). This will be explained in the discussion section, full workings are shown in appendix three. The reason for using the Mann-Whitney was because the data, although at interval level, didn't meet the full set of assumptions for a parametric test. Although the alone condition was a control condition it was included in the significant test. This means that there were three permutations for the simple and complex tasks. The table below shows the U values obtained from the Mann-Whitney.

It is necessary to explain why a particular test is appropriate, as is done here.

Table four shows the U values obtained from the Mann-Whitney significance test.

	Alone mere presence	Alone evaluation	Mere-presence evaluation
Simple task	49	42	41.5
Complex task	44	36.5	42

For the experimental hypothesis to be supported at the $p \leqslant 0.05$ level a U value of < 23 was needed. From the table above it can be seen that none of the conditions reached this, therefore the null hypothesis is supported. It is possible that a Type II error has been made.

Although findings may not support an experimental hypothesis, this does not mean that the hypothesis must be false. A Type II error may have been made.

Discussion

It was briefly mentioned in the results section that tables one and two clearly show from a simple 'eye-ball' test that the data collected go in the direction of the experimental hypothesis. That is to say, participants performed the simple task faster when they believed they were being evaluated, and performed the complex task slower. The range of times in the simple task show how participants produced a smaller range in the evaluation condition and larger in the alone, possibly demonstrating how strongly participants wanted to be judged as competent. In the complex task the range is more spread out as the more competent are still able to go faster but the less competent have to go more slowly to perform the task better. If the correlation's results are observed (graph two and three, and table three) then it can be seen that there isn't a significant trend between the amount of time it took participants to perform either the simple or complex task or the amount of mistakes made. This will be discussed later.

One interesting point to note in the results (shown clearly in graph one) is that in the mere-presence condition participants performed the simple task more slowly than in the evaluation condition. The experimenters had expected this to have been the reverse, as was shown on Schmitt's study. An initial theory could be to blame a fault in the procedure, but because there is no anomaly in the data for the complex task this is not borne out. Instead there may be another reason that explains this, in that another phenomenon may have appeared in the experiment. In the evaluation condition participants know what the other person in the room is doing (evaluating, because they are timing the participant), they therefore have a reason for the other person being in the room. But in the mere-presence condition participants are told to ignore the other person, and given no other details (in this experiment the 'other' person has their back to the participant, so they are facing a window and reading a book). When participants are performing the simple task they don't use their full cognitive processing potential and are therefore able to consider the 'other' person in the room, and despite wanting to produce a favourable image are slowed by this. In the complex task the mere-presence condition is again performed more slowly than the alone condition. In this case it may be more to do with the task as this would use up more of the individual's cognitive processing capacity.

This theory would need to be tested in a follow-up study. It might also be useful to ask participants what they perceive about the 'other' person to see if they were distracted by them. In this experiment it was found that several of the

An overall statement of the findings like this is very valuable. The graphs referred to here have not been reproduced, as the appendix to this report has been omitted for reasons of space.

When results do not go in the direction expected, particularly if it is contrary to other studies, then it is worth reviewing possible reasons. The writer does that effectively here.

This would be a useful modification of procedure.

participants were observed looking over at this person (this was seen covertly by the 'other' person watching the participants' reflection in the window). However, this is not a scientific approach because the reflection was not always present and the participant may have been looking 'through' the other person.

Despite the noticeable differences in the mean scores, the Mann-Whitney test did not produce a significant result at the experimental level of $P \leq 0.05$. This was a surprise considering the difference when participants performed the complex task in the alone condition and the evaluation condition (the total difference works out at 182 seconds or 18.2 seconds per participant). The insignificant result may be due to the type of test used, that is to say the Mann-Whitney is not very sensitive. Although the data do not meet the full assumptions of a parametric test, a t-test for unrelated data was performed between participants performing the complex task in the alone and evaluation condition (full workings are in appendix three). The test produced a t score of t=1.00. For the data to be significant at 0.05 the t score needed to equal or exceed 1.734, therefore the data are not significant.

The number of mistakes made by participants is interesting to note, particularly in the complex task. Allport (1920) found that in an evaluation condition participants performed at a faster rate than if they worked alone but they made more mistakes. In this experiment the opposite is true (table two). The difference though is slight; what has been found in this experiment to support Allport is that in the evaluation condition the faster participants went, the more mistakes they made (this produced a significantly positive correlation). One possible reason for participants not making more mistakes in the evaluation condition is a design incompatible with Allport's work. When the experimenters wrote the maths questions they did not want to make the questions too difficult. This was due to people's 'natural' fear of maths. What has been found in studies of arousal in areas such as emotion and attitude is that too much fear can actually inhibit performance and this would cause an extraneous variable creeping into the experiment; therefore the questions were not made very difficult. The fear of maths was highlighted by one participant who walked out on the maths question. The questions were made only to slow the participants down.

Helpful reference to earlier research.

As the aim of this study mentioned, this study reproduced Schmitt *et al.*'s experiment where they also had three conditions. The results produced show similar findings to the original experiment, thus supporting Cotterall's theory of evaluation apprehension. The results also give some support for Zajonc's drive theory, where he claims that even the mere presence of another person causes either facilitation or impairment. In this experiment both tasks were impaired by the other person. The main support (although not significant) of this practical is for Cotterall *et al.*'s theory. They found that if participants believed that they could be evaluated the performance dropped if the task was difficult (such as giving a speech in front of a higher-status audience). Although an audience was not used in this experiment, participants' performances dropped with the complex task.

One limitation of this study is that there was no measure of how the participants were feeling in any of the conditions. This may be important in determining the actual reason why the effect occurs. The measure may have linked the evaluation theory to Bond's presentation theory. In other words, the reason we are worried about being evaluated is that we want to look good in front of others. This means that we slow down our performance so that we make fewer mistakes in the complex task although this was not found to be so. But when doing the simple task we can go faster to give an equally good impression, and in fact this was found. In a follow-up study it may be appropriate to produce a simple questionnaire for participants to fill in, stating how they felt; for example, self-conscious. It could also incorporate the idea about how participants view the 'other' person.

Another adaptation to any future studies into this area could also be a physiological test measuring; for example, galvic skin resistance (GSR), heart rate and blood pressure. As mentioned in accordance with the maths question, participants may feel greater levels of arousal when performing the complex task, and this level of arousal could increase in the different condition, reaching the maximum in the evaluation condition. If this is used in conjunction with the questionnaire, then a stronger relation with the presentation theory may be formed.

> This would extend the scope of the experiment considerably. It might have other consequences on the results but would still be following the aim of the study.

One criticism with this experiment, apart from using an opportunity sample so that no generalisation can be made, is the rooms used for the experiment. The original intention of the experimenters was to use a room with a window in the door so that participants could be observed without realising it (the participant would have their back to the door). But because the sample was obtained from lecture groups at different times, different rooms were used. In one instance a room several floors up was used. This may have resulted in an extraneous variable getting into the design. This is because if arousal increased in the different conditions, participants in the group who had to climb more stairs would have already had a higher arousal state.

> A careful critique of the method used is always valuable. It may explain anomalies in results.

One important question that has to be asked is the matter of the experiment being reliable and valid – reliable in the sense that the same findings are produced on similar trials. Although the actual experiment differs from Schmitt's experiment it produces similar findings, and so the experiment appears reliable. The question of validity – that is, the test measures what it is supposed to measure – appears also to be borne out because an effect has appeared.

Conclusion

As stated at the start of the discussion section, the data produced were not significant, but do from a simple eye-ball test support the theory of Cotterall. Because of this the null hypothesis has been supported:

A final conclusion is helpful.

> There will be no significant difference between the time it takes participants to perform the simple and complex tasks if they believe they are being evaluated compared to being in the mere presence of another person.

Note: the appendices to this practical write-up were extensive and have been left out because of restrictions on space. They included further graphs and the full statistical workings for all the tests mentioned.

References

Adams Douglas, *The Hitch-hiker's Guide to the Galaxy.*
Heinemann: London.
Page 17 first paragraph. Used for the passage.
ISBN no: 0 434 00929 2

Baron and Byrne, *Social Psychology* (seventh edn).
Allyn & Bacon.
Pages 489–92 Definition of social facilitation, Zajonc's theory, Cotterall's theory and Schmitt's experiment.
ISBN no: 0 205 14883 2

Coolican, *Methods and Statistics in Psychology.*
Hodder & Stoughton.
Pages 190–3; Mann-Whitney test.
Pages 214–17; Spearman's rho.
Pages 203–5; t test.
ISBN no: 0 340 52404 9

Gross, *Principles of Psychology.*
Hodder & Stoughton.
Pages 554–5 Allport's (1920) observation of social facilitation.
ISBN no: 0 340 56136 x

Hayes, *Principles of Social Psychology.*
Lawrence Erlbaum Associates.
Pages 43–7; Bonds theory.
ISBN no: 0 86377 2595

Morison, *Essays and Practicals for Students*
Addison Wesley Longman.
Pages 70–74; How to write a practical.

Mark Stevenson

Revision and the examination

At various points during your course you will be revising for test essays. In preparation for the examination this process will begin in earnest. There are various techniques which you can use which will increase your effectiveness. Perhaps the main point to make is that *learning* your psychology notes and studies should not be left until a few weeks before the examination. As psychologists, you will appreciate that we remember best what we really understand. Rote learning is much less efficient. Consequently, you should see the revision process as being part of your course from the beginning. We will look at revision, surviving 'exam nerves' and making the best use of your time in the examination room.

Revision

Good notes

Your revision will be aided by having made good notes throughout your course. These should not be too detailed, but must be accurate. If set out neatly, with the intelligent use of colour for underlining and 'highlight' pens for the important parts, then they will be easier to learn from and recall. It is never too early to start making extra notes around a topic, to back up class work. The more familiar you are with material the easier it is to learn.

Regular review

You will find it very helpful, if throughout your course you devote a small amount of time, regularly, to reviewing your recent notes. We remember relatively little of any lecture we may have attended. However, if we read over the notes we have taken, then they become more firmly lodged in the memory. This review should be conducted ideally, each day and each week. It need only last a minute or two, because all you have to do is to bring the points back to your attention. It counteracts the process of 'decay' in the memory.

Card system

Many students find keeping a card system is very helpful. On each card a brief summary of the main points of specific studies or experiments is recorded. Small file cards are ideal. They may be used to revise from, and can ensure that you actually remember the key studies in the examination room, rather than having them on the 'tip of your tongue'.

Mnemonics

For many of the parts of the psychology syllabus, you will have to remember a series of studies or experiments. Often if you can recall the name of the experimenter, then the details will also come to mind. One simple technique is to come up with a mnemonic using the first letters of the names of psychologists. It is easier to recall one 'silly' word than eight or nine separate names. The process of working out a mnemonic also helps engrave the names on your memory. The figure overleaf shows how one enterprising student used the word 'perception' itself, to act as a memory jog. Using a summary sheet like this, with little pictures, can also be an effective way of revising. Pictures involve the imaging, or right side, of the brain. Putting pictures and ideas in a sequence means that we can move from one to the next by association. If you try out this technique (which rests on the same principle as the mind-maps used earlier in the book) you will discover that you can remember a sequence of material surprisingly effectively.

Plan for revision

The revision period should start several months prior to the examination. You should plan what you are going to revise and when, and draw up a schedule. Try to go over everything at least three times. The first time is to ensure that your notes are complete, and that you understand the ideas and the arguments. This phase is most important because you will not be able to learn material effectively that you do not understand. The second time you should put maximum effort into learning the material. Be ruthless with yourself, in checking that you really do recall the details of the studies and arguments that you have been learning. The third time is to check what you know, and to relearn what has not been memorised.

Be active

You will remember best what has gone actively through your mind. Don't just read through your notes. Close your file and verbally summarise (i.e., say out loud) the key ideas, or write them out. Make summaries of all the key points on a particular area, using boxes, colour, underlining, pictures, and any other techniques that will make them visually distinctive and memorable. Mind-maps would be particularly useful here as a way of drawing whole areas together in a structured way. Look at past questions, and either make detailed plans, or write out an answer in 43 to 45 minutes (the time available in the examination).

Work intensively for short periods separated by brief breaks. This maximises the primacy and recency effects, where we tend to remember best the beginnings and endings of activities.

PERCEPTION - ALL THE BITS YOU REALLY SHOULD KNOW!!

P — Perception in Psychology

Attention — selective

Memory

Person Perception — 1st impressions, Self, Attraction etc.

Conformity — look to leaders & authority. ex.- Attitudes

Child Development — look to significant others - now they behave. Also language acquisition

Nature v. Nurture Debate

Could also be involved in:
(i) Intelligence
(ii) aggression & prejudice
(iii) anxiety & stress
(iv) Emotion
(v) Learning
(vi) Motivation
(vii) Personality

BUT in real life you are not often presented with such situations!

I.E. you are not often confronted with ambiguous figures on a tachistoscope!

E — Expectation & Set

Ambiguous Figures

the letter B or the number 13? — MINTERN & BRUNER (1951)

Also

R — Readjustment Studies

How modifiable is Perception?

George Stratton (1897) Adapted after 8 days but then had to re-adapt.

Chickens did not adapt. But they would not have known what hit them!

So it isn't surprising really!

E.H. Hess (1956)

C — Cues ~ Secondary & Primary

Perception of depth — [BINOCULAR]
(i) difference of images in each eye — PRIMARY
(ii) convergence of eyes

[MONOCULAR] →
(i) change in lens shape — PRIMARY

(i) (x) (y)
(ii)
(iii)

(iv) Relative Brightness
(v) Aerial Perspective
(vi)
(vii)
(viii) Motion Parallax — SECONDARY

E — Effects of Values

We tend to perceive valued objects as larger than they really are (if value is associated with size)

Estimate coin size

50p — IOp — larger % & overestimation

Poor overestimation more

BRUNER & GOODMAN
10 Rich
10 Poor
10 Random
10 Year Olds

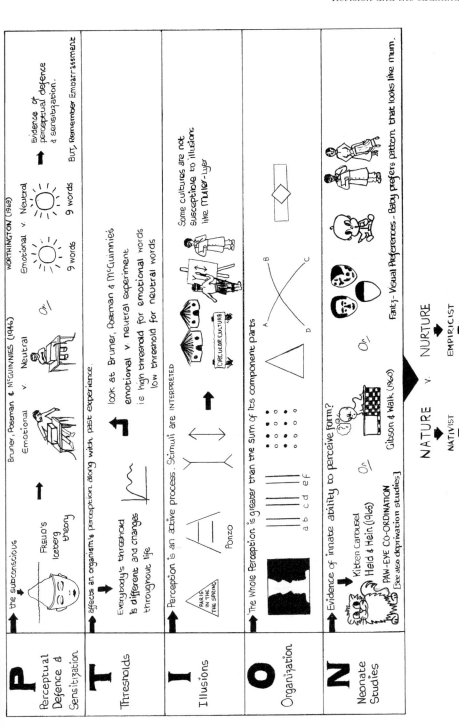

P Perceptual Defence & Sensitization

the subconscious → Freud's Iceberg theory

Bruner, Postman & McGuinnies (1946)
Emotional v. Neutral

WORTHINGTON (1969)
Emotional v. Neutral
9 words / 9 words
Evidence of perceptual defence & sensitization.
BUT, Remember Embarrassment.

T Thresholds

affects an organism's perception along with past experience.

Everybody's threshold is different and changes throughout life.

look at Bruner, Postman & McGuinnies emotional v neutral experiment
ie high threshold for emotional words
low threshold for neutral words

I Illusions

Perception is an active process. Stimuli are INTERPRETED

PARIS IN THE SPRING

Ponzo

CIRCULAR CULTURE

Some cultures are not susceptible to illusions like Müller-lyer

O Organisation

The Whole Perception is greater than the sum of its component parts

a b c d e f

A
B
C
D

N Neonate Studies

Evidence of innate ability to perceive form?

Kitten Carousel
Held & Hein (1963)
PAW-EYE CO-ORDINATION
[See also deprivation studies]

Gibson & Walk (1960)

Fantz - Visual Preferences - Baby prefers pattern that looks like mum.

NATURE v. NURTURE
NATIVIST   EMPIRICIST   J.Locke
Gestalt Psychologists
                D.O. Hebb

Preparing for the methodology question

By running through the questions given in this book (pages 137–140) you will cover most of the main concepts that are likely to occur in the examination. So be sure that you *understand* the answers to each of these questions. Similarly, work through all the past questions of this type and make sure you can answer each part. The statistical part of the syllabus is not that difficult to grasp, *if* you are prepared to give it enough time, and to think about the concepts. This book gives a summary of the main ideas but you will need also to go to one of the introductory specialist books on statistics.

Surviving 'exam nerves'

A bit of adrenaline is no bad thing in the examination, as it can sharpen concentration. Being so nervous that you cannot think straight is of no value at all. There are ways that you can help yourself feel calm on the day.

Relaxation

It is worth practising simple relaxation techniques for some months prior to the examination, so that it becomes a habit. There are several books readily available to teach you how to relax (e.g., Jane Madders, *Stress and Relaxation*).

Breathing

Slow deep breaths affect the body, and can help it to calm down when it is distressed. Take a few deep breaths before going into the exam. Do so again once you are in your place. The very act of stopping, thinking about your breathing, and allowing your body to relax, can help you to avoid making silly mistakes through panicking.

Affirmations

A simple psychological technique can assist in this area. If you find a little voice in your head informing you that you are likely to fail/forget/go blank and so on, just say 'STOP'. Then replace that voice with one you consciously choose, saying a phrase like 'I will remember everything I need to' or 'I will be clear-headed and calm in the exam'.

Sleep and exercise

The exam season is a stressful time. Regular exercise will help you survive it, and also help you sleep. An evening walk can be very beneficial – especially if you use it as a time for *not* thinking about work. Don't burn the 'midnight candle' too much; it is counterproductive.

Psychology examination checklist

Keep the following points in mind during the examination:

1 Read through the whole paper carefully.

2 Select your questions, making sure that you follow the rubric on the paper.

3 Spend *equal* time on each question, this usually means about 43 to 44 minutes each, after reading the questions through.

4 Underline the key words on the question. Do *not* copy the question out on to the answer sheet.

5 Make a brief plan.

6 Check that the plan answers the question.

7 Start your essay from a point relating to a key issue in the question.

8 Link your essay paragraph by paragraph. Also link the main points regularly back to the question. Keep the paragraphs fairly short.

9 Back up any arguments with relevant examples or experiments.

10 Put dates where appropriate.

11 Put studies in historical sequence unless you have good reason to do otherwise. In other words your answer should show the development of ideas and arguments.

12 If you find yourself running out of time – or of ideas – check if there is another 'angle' to follow:

theory/method

another 'model' (e.g., behaviourism, humanistic psychology, social learning theory etc.)

an issue (e.g., reductionism; free will *vs* determinism; idiographic or nomothetic; ethical consideration etc.)

animal studies, if relevant

13 If you run out of time then complete the last question giving points you would have covered in telegraphic form.

Statistics questions – guidance on answers

The answers given here are not model examination answers. Rather they are to help the student understand the content that must be covered in an examination answer. Generally what is required is a clear explanation, and an illustratio – either from the stimulus material provided or an example from a relevant situation.

Question 1

a) As they are frequency data, they can only be nominal.
b) The expected frequency is the score we would expect to obtain under the null hypothesis condition. In order to be valid it must equal or exceed five.
c) Degrees of freedom refers mathematically to the number of scores in a result that can be varied, whilst the *parameters* – in effect, the totals – remain the same. In this case, the *df* is 1. Do you know the formulae for computing the *df* for both a chi-square and a t-test?
d) It corrects for the error that can arise from using small samples, and *must* be used when the sample is under 25.
e) Here, '*p*' refers to the probability and '≤' can be expressed as 'equal to or less than'. A two-tailed test indicates that the experimenter does not predict the *direction* of the effect of the independent variable. Try putting both those ideas into a clear statement.
f) Descriptive statistics *describe* the data, whereas inferential statistics make *inferences* about the population that the sample (of people or scores) represents. It will be helpful to consider examples of both. One is looking back at the data already collected. The other, in effect, makes predictions. What is it making predictions about?

Question 2

a) Order effect, as the name suggests, is any extraneous influence produced by the order in which tests or activities are undertaken. Any possible effects need to be balanced out, or *counterbalanced*. You should be aware of how to do this when a group is undertaking more than two tests. Also, how should the group be allocated into sub-groups?
b) A Pearson's product moment test can only be applied when a scattergram indicates a straight line – not one that is curvilinear, or U-shaped.
c) A parametric test requires data that are of at least interval status,

normally distributed, and where both samples have a similar variance.
d) The significance level *is* the chance of making a Type I error, so, the chance is 5 in 10,000.
e) A Type II error is when a null hypothesis is accepted when it is false.
f) It is significant at the 0.025 level for a one-tailed test.

Question 3

a) The IV is whether the words are presented in categories or in random order. The DV is the number of words that are remembered under each condition.
b) The null hypothesis needs to reflect both the IV and the DV and to state that the group under the experimental condition (categories) will not have significantly different scores from the other group.
c) This refers to Popper's idea that in effect a scientist must test a conjecture (hypothesis) that is actually falsifiable. What is the implication if the hypothesis was *not* falsifiable?
d) There are two groups, randomly assigned rather than matched. So the design is *independent measures* or *between groups*.
e) Interval data, as the name suggests, are data that can be arranged on a scale of equal intervals. Test scores would usually be considered as interval. Ordinal data can, again as the name suggests, be put into rank order. Are interval data always ordinal?
f) Independent measures, testing for difference and with non-parametric data, hence Mann-Whitney.

Question 4

a) 34% or more accurately 34.15%.
b) The middle line, bisecting the highest point on the distribution is the mean, median and mode. What are the other characteristics of the normal curve of distribution?
c) Standard deviation is one measure of *dispersion*. In other words it is a measure of the average 'spread' of scores around the mean. It summarises the average score of all the scores around the mean of those scores. What is its relationship to the variance? And in this example, what is the variance?
d) This score will be 100. It is the mean plus two standard deviations.
e) The probability is 2.3 times in 100 or $p = .023$.

Question 5

a) The sampling frame is the school roll.
b) The overall population is most accurately the pupils at this school – i.e., the same as the sampling frame. However, the population could be all 11–16-year-old school children in this country. It

would depend how *representative* the school itself was of other schools.

c) A random sample means that extraneous variables will tend to cancel each other out. The random sample could be selected by taking every n^{th} name, by using random number tables or picking numbers that refer to the names, out of a hat.

Can you explain the difference between extraneous variables and confounding variables?

d) Demand characteristics are the inferences which the subject picks up about the purpose of the experiment and what is expected of him or her. In this case what might the pupils infer about the purpose of the experiment? How might this influence their response?

e) Two tests of reliability are the *test–retest* method and the *split–half* test. These would need to be explained.

f) Validity is when a test measures *truthfully*. In other words it measures what it is supposed to measure. It is the adequacy of a test to address the issue it is meant to address. This can be assessed in terms of its content, its results with known groups and its predictive ability. Consistency is not, in itself, a measure of validity, but of reliability. So a reliable test *may* be consistently invalid!

Question 6

a) In this experiment your participants perform under two conditions. This is therefore a *repeated measures* design.

b) You cannot assume that the attitude scale is treated by the subjects in the same way, nor that the steps between scores are of equal value. Hence, the data are only of *ordinal* status, because you can put them in rank order.

c) The experimental hypothesis must include the IV and the DV and specify the relationship between them. In this case the IV is the soap operas, and the DV is the rating given to them. As you are unsure which will prove more popular, you just need to specify that there will be a significant difference in the scores on the attitude scale. The hypothesis therefore has to be two-tailed.

d) The level of significance achieved for a two-tailed test is always half that for a one-tailed test. In other words, if it is of borderline significance for a two-tailed test, it will be significant for a one-tailed test.